Library of
Davidson College

SAGE CONTEMPORARY SOCIAL SCIENCE ISSUES 26

POLITICAL PARTICIPATION UNDER MILITARY REGIMES

Edited by
Henry Bienen
and
David Morell

SAGE PUBLICATIONS *Beverly Hills / London*   1976

The material in this publication originally appeared as a special issue of ARMED FORCES AND SOCIETY (Volume 1, Number 3, Spring 1975); the article by Philippe Schmitter was published in the Fall 1975 issue (Volume 1, Number 4) of the same journal. Reprinted with the permission of the Inter-University Seminar on Armed Forces and Society. Sage Publications, Inc. would like to acknowledge the assistance of the General Editor, Morris Janowitz, and the special issue editors, Henry Bienen and David Morell, in making this edition possible.

Copyright © 1975 by Inter-University Seminar on Armed Forces and Society. This edition first published Spring 1976.

All rights reserved. No part of this book may be reproduced or utilized in any form or by any means, electronic or mechanical, including photocopying, recording, or by any information storage and retrieval system, without permission in writing from the publisher.

For information address:

SAGE PUBLICATIONS, INC.
275 South Beverly Drive
Beverly Hills, California 90212

SAGE PUBLICATIONS LTD
St George's House / 44 Hatton Garden
London EC1N 8ER

Printed in the United States of America

International Standard Book Number 0-8039-0584-x

Library of Congress Catalog Card Number 75-32376

FIRST PRINTING

CONTENTS

Preface
MORRIS JANOWITZ — 5

Alternatives to Military Rule in Thailand
DAVID MORELL — 9

Transition from Military Rule: *The Case of South Korea*
C.I. EUGENE KIM — 24

Civilianization of Military Regimes in the Arab World
GABRIEL BEN-DOR — 39

Transition from Military Rule: *The Case of Western State Nigeria*
HENRY BIENEN — 50

Civilian Participation Under Military Rule in Uganda and Sudan
NELSON KASFIR — 66

Liberation by *Golpe: Retrospective Thoughts on the Demise of Authoritarian Rule in Portugal*
PHILIPPE SCHMITTER — 86

Review Article

The Liberation Army and the Chinese People
LYNN T. WHITE III — 115

Preface

This volume consists of papers devoted to a crucial theme, namely, the analysis of political participation under military regimes. It represents the work of a group of political scientists who are concerned whether military regimes can or will "exit from political power." They attack this fundamental issue by means of a series of case studies informed by contemporary theory in political science and organizational analysis.

These papers are the product of scholars with strong expertise in the geographical areas of their particular interest. However, Henry Bienen and David Morell, who have organized this collection of research papers, are able to present findings which should be of interdisciplinary interest to students of military organization, civil-military relations, and the processes of social and political change in the developing nations. They offer an overview and analysis of the realities and dilemmas which military regimes face. This issue is therefore part of the continuing effort in the interdisciplinary approach of the Inter-University Seminar on Armed Forces and Society.

Henry Bienen and David Morell are interested in the conditions under which military regimes withdraw from political power and hopefully establish stable and competitive political systems. More generally, under what conditions do military regimes transform themselves into civilian governments of lasting duration? Military regimes have a powerful reluctance to give up political power, although in the process of exercising authority they face deep and disruptive dilemmas. Therefore, the papers assembled by Henry Bienen and David Morell recast the issue from a narrow discussion of "the exit from power" to a broader examination of the mixed systems of military and civilian politics, which have become widespread in the third world. The underlying conclusion of these papers is that the form of political participation which military regimes permit and encourage directly influences the extent and viability of the trend toward the civilianization of military regimes.

In the nation states of Africa, the Middle East, and the Far East, the rise to power of the military regimes does not mean the cessation of group politics—informal or organized. These regimes are authoritarian and they operate with constricted limits on the political opposition. However, they hardly conform to the totalitarian model of industrialized nations. To the contrary, military regimes frequently seek to encourage new patterns of political participation if they are committed to the goal of a return to civilian rule. In their search for popular support and political legitimacy, they must often seek alliances with existing political groupings. Their desire to persist in power brings about a transformation in which military regimes struggle for accommodation with civilian notables which can produce fragmented patterns of political participation. Moreover, there have been sufficient cases of a return to civilian rule—if only temporarily— which exposed the extent of civilian political participation under military rule.

It is now almost a decade since the first serious writing on the military in the "new nations" appeared. Social science perspectives have matured and the passage of time has supplied the materials in depth for the analysis of the role of the military in political change. The focus of attention has shifted from an analysis of the conditions and causes of the seizure of power to an assessment of the performance of military regimes and mixed forms of military-civilian governments. But the initial formulations of this basic issue have a striking persistence. Over a decade ago, one group of writers stressed the potentials of military regimes and military personnel for enhancing the process of socio-political "modernization." The alternative approach was to anticipate limitations and difficulties under military rule, and to emphasize the relevance of the process of civilianization.

Of course, individual military regimes have produced records of economic growth, but not without a high price of political instability or repression. Thus, the latter formulation of a decade ago which stressed the dilemmas and political fragility of military regimes is strongly supported by the contents of these research papers. These case studies document the wide range of efforts of military regimes to develop civilian alliances. They highlight the stubborn resistance of military elites when civilian groups press for enlarged political power. As a result, Henry Bienen and David Morell are able to emphasize that a sharp distinction between military and civilian regimes is an oversimplification. Instead, we have witnessed the emergence of varying types of mixed regimes—under which the military most generally retains the final authority.

The case studies are drawn from widely ranging geographical areas and different political histories. They can all be juxtaposed to the Ataturk model—the specific case of Turkey in the 1920s and 1930s, in which the Turkish military leader created a single mass party under the domination of the military. The personnel of this mass party were gradually separated from the military officer group. The mass party in time lost a contested election to the political opposition, although over the long run the military reserved the right to intervene.

David Morell's analysis focuses on the very different set of circumstances in Thailand. In that nation state, the repeated retreat from power by the military involved a partial transfer of power to highly fragmented civilian groups. The result thus far has been the return to military intervention after each effort at civilian regimes.

South Korea is analyzed by C. I. Eugene Kim as a case which has closely paralleled the Ataturk model. The process of civilianization of the military regime has produced a mass civilian party under the domination of the military leadership. This political apparatus has been repeatedly successful in quasi-competitive elections. But progressively, the impact of international affairs has led toward a more and more authoritarian regime, so that the objectives of civilianization have not been attained.

The analysis of military rule in Egypt and Syria and other Arab states by Gabriel Ben-Dor rests on the distinction between abrupt and gradual civilianization of military regimes. In this area of the world, the impact of international relations and military conflict creates the base for the persistence of military intervention in domestic politics. But the necessity of political support in the management of national affairs has led to a gradual process of civilianization in nations such as Egypt and Syria. The format that results leaves the military as the key element in the socio-political balance, while not overlooking the additional elements of civilian support which are essential for maintenance of political dominance by any particular leader.

There are military regimes which seek to deal with their political dilemmas by announcing that in the future there will be a national election to form a civilian regime. The prospect of a national election intensifies civilian political participation. Since the outcome of such elections are unclear, and the danger of a highly fragmented result is ever present, it is not surprising that military regimes, reluctant to give up power, often postpone the dates of promised elections. Henry Bienen's field research in Nigeria deals with such a set of circumstances. His analysis traces out the complex pattern of civilian participation which was generated by the military regime in Western Nigeria. The case of Nigeria highlights the extent to which this military regime relies on former administrative personnel, and the profound hostility and distrust of the former political leaders toward the military government. Given the gulf between the military elites and the active political civilian leaders, the abrupt exit from power by the military is seen as remote.

The dilemmas and difficulties of stimulating local roots civilian participation are similarly highlighted by the study prepared by Nelson Kasfir of such efforts in Uganda and Sudan. In the case of Uganda, the whole personality of General Amin, the internal social tension, and the high level of border tensions quickly ended the experimentation with grass-roots political participation. By contrast, Sudan presents the case in which the military regime has been more persistent in the search for forms of local citizen participation, both to supply an element of popular support and in order to reduce the threat of internal strife.

Philippe Schmitter examines the conditions under which the military in Portugal became the active center of a revolt against the civilian dictatorial regime. In particular, his analysis bears on the central issue of political participation under military rule because in this case the military regime developed a leftist faction. This left wing component set the arena for the patterns of political participation and violence in the subsequent period of military rule.

The book review article by Lynn White presents the opportunity to assess the case of mainland China as a developing nation with powerful military institutions. White underlines the difficulties of analyzing Chinese institutions in terms of the categories of civil-military relations formulated in the West, because of the deep interpenetration of the armed forces and the political apparatus of the state. However, it may well be the case that China does have parallels with the format of a mixed regime so typical in the third world. In this case, the roles are reversed, with the civilians in control, but dependent on the vitality of the armed forces for their political dominance. The impending issues and tensions connected with leadership succession bring into focus the powerful impact of the armed forces on the internal politics of Communist China.

This volume on the topic of armed forces and society is a contribution to a refashioning of perspective in research on civil-military relations in the developing nations. It is more and more apparent that the underlying question is not the conditions under which the military will "exit from power" but rather how the long and twisted process of the transformation of the military regimes will take place. What are the elements which speed up or retard the process of civilianization, and fashion the patterns of civilian political participation? The term institution-building has some pointed relevance since it does not require the use of Western parliamentary institutions as the basic criterion of assessment. In any case, military regimes have come into power in many developing nations only after the breakdown of parliamentary institutions. The search continues, as it has for over a decade, for the construction of political arrangements which will not immediately fragment, and which therefore will lead to increased military intervention with even greater reliance on coercion and with unanticipated consequences.

—*Morris Janowitz*

Alternatives to Military Rule in Thailand

DAVID MORELL
Princeton University

Thailand's political metamorphosis over the past four decades, beginning with the military intervention of June 24, 1932, after centuries of rule by absolute monarchy, provides an example of politics dominated by competition between strong, unified armed forces and aspiring civilian leaders, each seeking personal and institutional access to principal authority. Civil-military relations have been a critical factor in all periods of military and occasional civilian rule. When the military was hegemonic (during some 35 of the past 42 years) and ruled through martial law decrees, pressures for some transition to civilian leadership were unceasing; constitutional forms, elections, political parties, and interventionist legislatures periodically emerged as alternatives to absolute military rule, all within a rubric of monarchical political legitimacy and patron-client tactical maneuvering. Similarly, during the much briefer and often turbulent periods of civilian rule, the dominant power reality has remained the military's intentions: would the army intervene once again to reestablish military rule and to end another transition attempt, and how would the military behave when they returned to power?

Although one postwar period of transition from military rule in Bangkok, lasting from July 1944 to November 1947,[1] offers certain insights into the transition phenomena, the two attempts to institutionalize the transition process—(1) June 1968 to November 1971; and (2) October 1973 to the present[2]—are the subject of this paper. Both of these periods manifest notable similarities with, as well as important differences from, the classic Ataturk transition model; there are also some important differences between the two Thai cases themselves. Both periods witnessed reintroduction of a "democratic" constitution, popular election of a national parliament,[3] and emergence of political parties. To some degree the constitutions protected civil liberties from the worst excesses of martial law and military rule,[4] but in both cases the parliament's inherent powers have been circumscribed by the authority of the executive branch.

Some rather unique characteristics of the Thai situation provide the basis for that nation's transition experience to date, and suggest caution in drawing generalizations from the Thai model. Foremost are the tandem influences of the monarchy and the absence of a colonial heritage. The royalty in Thailand continues to perform vital political functions, particularly as the source of legitimacy, cohesive national identity, and politically relevant social status. The fragmentation of ethnic/political components and the quest for a modicum of legitimacy so typical of most developing polities simply are not major problems for Thailand. The continuing importance and inherent power of the monarchy in Thai politics place distinct constraints on the military, limiting the degree to which a military leader can exercise national charisma and rendering the armed forces liable to the palace for continuing recognition of their legitimate political role. The king's cessation of this recognition in 1973, seen as necessary to quell student dissidence and to punish military intransigence and brutality, brought down the Thanom/Praphat regime.

In addition, of course, Thailand is unusual since it escaped colonization. From the perspective of transition from military rule, this has meant that the typical model of a weak parliamentary and party system collapsing after independence, with the military taking over, simply does not fit the Thai case. The military coup of 1932, rather than a thrust to independence from colonial rule, brought the country its first constitution, replacing absolute monarchy and rule by the princes with constitutional monarchy and rule by the praetorians. Ever since, Thai politics has remained elite politics, a post-1932 version of palace intrigue. In their attempts to cope with the transition challenge, Thai military leaders have never selected the Ataturk model of creating a mass party under their direct domination; instead they have turned over power to (or acquiesced in the accrual of power by) fragmented civilian political groups. The result continues to be a highly unstable political outcome. Other significant characteristics of the Thai situation include the high degree of racial homogeneity of the populace, combined with a rather well-integrated overseas Chinese minority; a continued tolerance for paternalistic authoritarianism in the political culture; and an increasing gap between urban (Bangkok) and rural polities.

The most profound differences between the 1968-1971 and post-October 1973 transitions emanate from their political genesis and personal characteristics of top national leaders. The peaceful, ultimately unsuccessful transition initiated in mid-1968 was engendered and led by the same group of generals who had dominated Thai politics since the mid-1950s. In contrast to the Turkish and South Korean cases, Field Marshals Thanom Kittikachorn and Praphat Charusathien, along with the other top military leaders, did not resign their military positions. Thus, the army's role remained paramount throughout the transition period, and the executive structure dominated the parliament through manipulation of a government political party.

Thailand's most recent transition experience, by contrast, emerged from the violent events of October 1973, when a student-led demonstration succeeded in forcing the top military leadership to resign from office and to flee the country.[5] The subsequent prime minister, Dr. Sanya Thammasak, is a civilian ex-judge, rector of Thammasat University, and member of the Privy Council, as well as a close personal acquaintance of King Phumiphon. In contrast to military leaders of other periods, Sanya is presiding over the initial phases of a transition process that he has no intention of directing; after the February 1975 election he plans to relinquish power to a new prime minister.

The army's political role in 1974 has been far less evident than in 1968-1971, and although the potential for reintervention certainly exists, numerous constraints operate which keep the military temporarily in a "wait-and-see" posture.

PRINCIPAL ISSUES IN TRANSITION, 1968-1971

A constitution was promulgated in June 1968, and political parties emerged to contest the February 1969 national election, the first in over a decade. Reflecting military dominance over the transition process, the new constitution established several constraints on the legislature's chances to become a powerful institution. An appointed Senate stood as the primary representative of the executive branch, a counterweight to the elected House. Prior to election of the Lower House, 164 Senators (three-fourths the number of elected representatives) were appointed by the king, who in essence named individuals selected by Thanom, Praphat, and the military cabinet. Since vital items of legislation required either Senate approval per se or a two-thirds majority in a joint session of both Houses, this maneuver ensured the military group's continuance in power. Other constitutional constraints on legislative influence included:

- stipulation that MPs could not be appointed to ministerial positions, thus avoiding the need for cabinet aspirants to stand for election;
- limitation on the elected House's power to implement general debates leading to a vote of non-confidence; and
- specification of executive tenure at four years, coterminous with the tenure of the elected House, but separate from the six-year Senate term.[6]

Even with these restrictions, the elected House of Representatives and its members managed to wield considerable influence over the political process. During the 33 months of its existence, the legislature had a surprisingly important impact on government policies, decisions, and actions. Representatives intervened wherever possible in the budget process, shifting allocations from one category to another and delaying passage of the budget bill for several months each year. They forced the cabinet to rescind major portions of its tax increase proposal announced by royal decree in mid-1970, altered the locations of many economic development projects, argued for greater attention to village-level development and small-scale improvement projects, and demanded and received access to provincial development funds for use at their own discretion. Their pressure for an equitable Press Control Act and opposition to the cabinet's proposals in this regard caused the measure to be delayed indefinitely. Elected representatives strongly opposed changes in the judicial structure proposed by the cabinet, eventually compelling the leaders to withdraw their proposal, forced reassignment of the powerful budget director, and shifted control over the central fund (for one year) to the Ministry of Finance. They attempted (unsuccessfully) to force the foreign minister to resign, compelled the Ministry of Interior to reassign several district officers and police commanders, and led the battle to wrest the controversial power of criminal investigation away from the police. Though many were themselves "on the take," MPs enthusiastically exposed cases of bureaucratic corruption. Several elected representatives were active in the foreign policy field, expressing their views and acting independently from the executive branch. Finally, and most important of all, representatives made it their chief business to discover and to articulate the views, interests, and serious needs of their rural constituents, bringing them to the attention of the Bangkok power elite.

In the aggregate, this parliamentary activity—or legislative intervention—proved a great annoyance to the military elite and its bureaucratic allies. It was a threat to the elite's continued ability to unilaterally make and to implement decisions, a role to which they were not only accustomed, but which they considered their right and private business. MPs aggressively demanded authority and influence over government programs, policies, and decisions, and set forth a barrage of information on rural problems which the bureaucracy did not care to receive. But since they operated from such an inherently weak base of power, with minimal legitimacy and negative status, their constantly escalating demands—aggravated by severe problems of factional competition with the cabinet in the fight for political succession eventually ensured their downfall. For a while, the open political system was able to operate on bureaucratic inertia and military tolerance, while leaders relied on cooptation, corruption, and traditional patron-client relationships to keep parliamentary interference at a manageable level; but by 1971 the pendulum of Thai politics had swung back again. MP-initiated proposals deferred for two or three years could no longer be smothered in "national security" rhetoric, threats to bureaucratic corruption and privilege increased as representatives demanded additional development funds in return for their continued support of cabinet proposed legislation, and the national election due in early 1973 loomed ever larger on the horizon.

It is impossible to isolate one cause for the resumption of military rule on November 17, 1971. There were many demands on the political system: from impatient MPs; from frightened urbanites; from bureaucrats wanting to expedite passage of their legislative proposals; from cliques favoring new or old foreign policies; from younger military leaders competing for present power and for advantageous positions in political struggles to come. These demands far exceeded the capacities of the political system, and by November 1971 military leaders had determined that the only way to handle the parliament was to discard it. The political system had again failed to institutionalize political parties and related participant structures, the rural mass was not yet sufficiently mobilized or politicized, and the vast majority of the population, not surprisingly, evidenced no signs of dismay when bureaucratic and military leaders decided to return to the 1958-1968 style of military rule.

The strengths and weaknesses of the government's Saha Pracha Thai (SPT) party were crucial to the potential success and ultimate failure of the 1969-1971 transition attempt. Traditionally, Thai political parties have been weak, loose aggregations of personalistic factions reflecting the patron-client nature of power relationships in the bureaucratic polity.

Party cohesion, loyalty, and discipline generally have been non-existent, and elected MPs have shifted with alacrity from one party to another.

The SPT party's performance in 1969-1971 was a microcosm of civil-military relations in the broader political arena. Its leaders, who retained their dominance over the cabinet and the armed forces, attempted to use the government party as the principal institutional mechanism for pursuing electoral/legislative politics. The party was well financed; it had a flexible, forward-looking constitution and rules of procedure, but although it was an amalgam of the most important political figures in the kingdom, the party was unable to escape the endemic factional competition, battling over candidate selection, control over party decisions, and support from the party's elected contingent. The focus of party leaders' activity remained internal; they competed against one another rather than pulling together to mobilize the citizenry. Unwilling to use the party's MPs as a mechanism for participant mobilization, they chose to rely on the tried, trusted, and understood techniques of bribery, patronage, coercion, and corruption to keep their supporters in line and to improve their own base of support at the expense of factional opponents. Finally, the SPT party was a bifurcated structure: party leaders (primarily military) versus the elected parliamentary contingent (civilian). Interaction, competition, conflict, and cooperation between these two groups were the principal machinery of politics in the SPT, as in the broader political system. And in both cases, the balance of political power was of course on the side of the military leadership.

As a political institution, the SPT party proved unable to fulfill its principal requirement: providing an effective mechanism for continued rule by the military elite and their bureaucratic supporters in a constitutional environment. The party reflected the problems of the political system as a whole. Failure to institutionalize a constitutive system in the 1969-1971 period was the result of attitudes and goals characteristic of the entire military/bureaucratic complex, as over and over again the party's parliamentary contingent proved unwilling to subordinate the interests of rural constituents—and their own personal ambitions—to party leaders' goals of political stability and maintenance of the status quo. Too many of the representatives' demands were perceived by party leaders as unsuitable, and by pushing these demands with ever greater intensity, they precipitated the demise of the transition attempt itself.

PRINCIPAL ISSUES IN TRANSITION, POST-OCTOBER 1973

The events of October 1973 presented a unique opportunity to expand civilian control over the armed forces, to consolidate this control through changing political attitudes, institutions, and relationships, and to effect at last a transition to civilian leadership backed by more than a minority of intellectuals and hopeful politicians. The army was deeply discredited by its response to student demonstrations, which had involved shooting into unarmed crowds and causing hundreds of casualties. Political legitimacy was transferred immediately and explicitly by the king from the armed forces to respected civilians, if not to the students and their leaders who had initiated the revolution. Thanom, Praphat, and Narong were forced into exile abroad, causing an almost total restructuring of patron-client linkages at the top of the political hierarchy. Dr. Sanya's primary political objectives upon assuming the prime ministership (the first civilian to hold the office in 15 years) definitely included presiding over a peaceable but firm transition from military rule. Although Thailand's latest transition attempt is still in its infancy, enough evidence does exist to assess whether realistic alternatives to military rule exist or whether civilian control shall remain a myth.

In the immediate aftermath of the October violence, a number of critical issues faced the Thai political system: formation of a new cabinet; restructuring political and patron-client relationships in the absence of the three departed military leaders; deciding the relative political roles of the king, armed forces, bureaucracy, and the new student elements; and refurbishment of the constitution, legislature, and political parties as the institutional manifestations of the structure for transition to a new civilian regime. Almost immediately, Prime Minister Sanya, in consultation with the palace and student leaders, appointed an eighteen-member committee to prepare a draft constitution in six months. The draft document, actually completed in January 1974, primarily reflected the views of progressive elements who had heightened access to power after the October revolution. Several of its provisions were in sharp contrast to the 1968 constitution. Fundamental changes were made in procedures for selection of the cabinet and the Upper House. Under the new system established in the draft constitution, there was again to be a bicameral National Assembly. The House of Representatives was to be directly elected; its members would then elect the Senate instead of having appointments made by the king as in 1968. Any military or civilian official elected to either house would have to resign his executive branch position, a major innovation to effect separation of powers.[7] The prime minister and all members of the cabinet, who were to be selected by the assembly and then appointed by the king, must be members of the National Assembly (either house), another change from previous practice and one which would increase political accountability of top national leaders. Another innovation was a requirement for the proposed new constitution to be approved by public vote in a national referendum prior to its promulgation by the king—an unprecedented recognition of popular sovereignty over the constitutional process.

The leaders of the student revolution and the new civilian government were unwilling to have the draft constitution submitted for review and approval to the old National Assembly established by the since-discredited military leaders. Here, too, an innovative approach was chosen when the National Convention, composed of 2,436 members appointed by the king, was formed to elect 299 members of a new National Assembly, one which would approve the new constitution and would serve as a parliament until nationwide elections could be held. But several differences in the relative proportions of these two bodies indicate the inability of the progressive forces which led the October revolution to consolidate their power over the political system. For example, local leaders from rural areas comprised 27% of the larger, earlier group, by far the largest single category; they accounted for only 5% of the National Assembly. Civil servants, predominantly from the Ministry of Interior, formed the largest single group in the assembly (33%), as compared to 13% in the convention. Unwilling to insist on overt leadership roles, deferring to their elders, and lacking a senior leader of their own who would be willing to coalesce the many disparate elements into a cohesive force, student and civilian leaders presented a dismaying show of internal factionalism, polarization, personal conflicts, and, as a result of all these, failure to produce a movement. Instead of moving with sufficient determination to exploit their unique advantages, they abdicated power to older conservative elements such as Sanya and the bureaucratic power brokers. This failure, symbolized in the composition of the National Convention and National Assembly, became even clearer when the days of decision on the new constitution dawned; the fragmented nature of the political parties which had been formed was depressingly obvious to everyone.

Under scrutiny by the National Assembly, several profound modifications were made in the draft constitution and its structural format for transition from military rule. The Senate, as in the 1969-1971 period, was now to be appointed by the king rather than indirectly elected by the House of Representatives. This would ensure dominance of the Senate by civilian bureaucrats and military officers, just as in the past, thereby isolating the elected House from the remainder of the political system. The cabinet, under the revised constitution, was to be composed "not more than half from outside the National Assembly," as opposed to the original draft which required the prime minister and his *entire* cabinet to be members of the assembly. Now half the ministers could be selected directly from the armed forces, bureaucracy, or business community, with the other half presumably coming predominantly from the appointed Senate rather than the elected House. Thus was defeated the attempt to achieve increased political accountability for the nation's political leaders, and they would not, after all, have to be linked—even indirectly—to the general public through the electoral process. Equally significant was the decision by the National Assembly to delete the referendum provisions included in the draft constitution, both for popular approval of the constitution itself and for selected items of legislation thereafter, destroying another potentially potent link between the body politic and the Bangkok power elite which the drafting committee had hoped to establish.

A large number of political parties emerged since 1973 to participate in the latest transition attempt. Fragmentation and factionalism are again endemic; the contrast with the 1969-1971 period is particularly evident with former MPs who were associated with the government party in the earlier phase of parliamentary politics. In place of a single government party, former SPT MPs have split into three competing groups: the Thai Nation party, the Social Agriculture party, and the Buddhist Socialist party. Each of these groups is supported by certain leading military officers as well as civilian bureaucrats and former elected representatives. The 1975 election will be the first in which the government in power (the cabinet) has not fielded its own political party. Sanya has decided not to do this, playing instead a neutral "overseer" role.

Other important parties entering (or reentering) the political arena in 1974 include: (1) the new Social Action party (SAP), led by the intellectual and journalist M. R. Kukrit Pramoj, Speaker of the National Assembly; (2) the Democrat party, the nation's oldest, along with a factional off-shoot called the Democracy party; (3) the New Force party, closest in many ways to the goals expressed in the wake of the October 1973 revolution; and (4) the United Socialist Front, the only truly socialist party in the group. The student groups and their leaders, themselves fragmented into competing factions, have chosen not to affiliate with any of these parties; and this further isolates student elements from the attempt to institutionalize a transition from military rule.

Since it seems certain that the next election will not produce a clear House majority for any single party, some type of coalition government will be required. The leader of whichever party gains the largest number of seats in the House will probably become prime minister, although someone else might emerge in an attempt to forge a broader compromise. Given the fragmentation and polarization which already exist well in advance of the rhetoric expected in a hotly contested campaign, such a coalition will be difficult to achieve, producing a high potential for political instability and a consequent rationale for military intervention. Polarization is evident in the fact that no one group effectively occupies the center. Both SAP and the Democrat party would like to do so, but in fact neither does, and further polarization and destabilization seem likely to occur in the House after the election.

During 1974, the military's morale and sense of mission were at their lowest ebb since the end of World War II, and so it used the bad year as a period of quiet, watchful waiting to determine whether civilians would indeed be able to consolidate their unexpected new positions of power. Although some individual senior military officers—both active commanders and retired generals—developed relationships with new political parties, their leverage was constrained by the army's institutional weakness and wariness, and by the wisdom of remaining top military officers.

Thailand's latest attempt at transition from military rule has been almost entirely a civilian enterprise, while the army remained an ominous but quiescent "eminence grise," watching from the shadows. A cohesive civilian government with active political parties forming an effective coalition cabinet could combine continued legitimacy from the monarchy with new sources of legitimacy from the electoral, representational process, thereby precluding overt military intervention for the foreseeable future. On the other hand, if a fragmented set of competing civilian groups, lacking leadership and unable to preside over a period of heightened instability, leads the nation into an era of economic disaster and social disorganization, the army will not hesitate to provide once again the "strength" and "decisiveness" which have been its trump cards in the past.

Transition from military rule in Thailand is dependent on effecting mutually beneficial political interactions between the monarchy and emerging extra-bureaucratic institutions. However, this need not mean that the king would actively "play politics," thereby sacrificing the sanctity of his position and possibly jeopardizing continuance of the dynasty. The palace does interact extensively with the military, bureaucracy, and business community; similar techniques and mechanisms could be devised for royal interaction with participant political institutions.

More is involved than the formal tasks of opening a new parliamentary session or presiding over ceremonies commemorating Constitution Day. Public statements are one possibility, with the king publicly encouraging "good men" to stand for election. He could reemphasize the importance of political participation and of honest, free elections; openly castigate those involved in political corruption, in the bureaucracy as well as in the parliament; stress grievance articulation and fair, equitable treatment of all Thai citizens by the bureaucracy. But of equal importance are the king's personal contacts with those men and women who take the risky step of entering electoral politics. If the king spoke with praise and optimism of such activities; invited representatives to social functions at the palace; asked for periodic briefings from leaders of different political parties on the issues of the day and the various policy alternatives which they were advocating; asked elected representatives to accompany the royal family on visits to the provinces—if the king indicated in a variety of open and subtle ways that these politicians were engaged in tasks of importance to the future of the kingdom—the public at large and the royalty-conscious elite would begin to change their minds about the legislative institution and its place in the Thai political system. And all this could be accomplished at essentially no cost to the monarchy.

The king provided very little of this kind of support to the transition attempt between 1968 and 1971. He did intervene personally in October 1973 to end the violence by ordering Thanom, Praphat, and Narong into exile, then selecting Sanya as prime minister and naming members of the National Convention, but whether he will provide the necessary support and legitimacy for transition in 1975 remains to be seen.

LESSONS FROM THAILAND'S TRANSITION EXPERIENCE

Although the specific features of moving from a political process dominated by the armed forces to one in which civilian leaders and non-military institutions serve as the principal decision makers will vary considerably from one political system to another, several apparent commonalities emerge from Thailand's experience.

The feature of greatest single importance is civilian weakness, not military strength. If civilian leaders and non-military institutions are embroiled in bickering and factional competition, transition from a military regime cannot succeed. This is true whatever the extent of manpower or weaponry available to the armed forces. If civilians—probably the largest residual category in the social sciences—are unable to pull themselves together and to devise coherent structures for national governance, the resultant chaos and instability produce a power vacuum into which the armed forces quickly move; this is the fundamental lesson of the Thai experience.

Students of armed forces and society concerned with the transition process, therefore, must assess why civilian political structures are weak as well as why armies are strong. The length of military rule, the degree to which the military has coopted or subverted potential rivals, inherent divisions between various civilian groups, and the nature of the military's own strategy for rule all enter into this equation. The outcome for the political process of a high degree of fragility of civilian rule must be evaluated. Similarly, political leaders in developing countries facing the transition challenge must devote attention to development of effective political parties which reach beyond the capital city into the provincial periphery; to creation of relatively powerful legislative institutions which offer a modicum of access for demand articulation, political participation, and grievance resolution; and to procedures to improve the capabilities of the civil bureaucracy as a principal institution for governance and interaction between governors and the governed.[8]

The Thai experience underlines the complexity of civil-military relations and the subsequent importance of crosscutting alliances between various military and non-military groups. Neither the armed forces nor the non-military components of the power structure are monolithic, and each tends to be fragmented into factions and groups which compete with one another for power and influence. In all developing countries, the armed forces divide by service categories: army, navy, air force (and, often, national police). In addition, within the army (almost always the politically relevant force) there are splits between line commanders and staff officers; between academy and non-academy graduates; between those with overseas training and experience and those whose entire careers have been in the indigenous community; between active duty and retired officers; between those who see the army's role as inherently political and those who are more concerned about defense capabilities per se; between officers whose primary concerns involve domestic politics and policies and those who have become more involved in the nation's foreign policies; and between those officers who are committed to supporting a successful transition from military rule and those who oppose the process and press for continued military dominance. Furthermore, other army groupings emerge around particular personalities, as patron-client mechanisms competing with one another for budgetary resources, assignments, promotions, status, and access to key decisions. Similarly, many identifiable subcategories emerge in the non-military arena. Of particular importance are career senior civil servants (e.g., the under-secretaries) in various ministries, and especially the Ministry of Interior; key decision makers in the Office of the Prime Minister, especially in the Budget Bureau and Economic Planning Agency; leaders of various political parties, particularly their elected components in the legislature; businessmen, bankers, labor leaders, and other economic interest groups; students and intellectuals; and, in the Thai context, the monarchy.

If a transition attempt were succeeding, one would expect to see an extensive series of complex alliances between various sets of military and civilian political actors, each forming a combined civil-military group. Conversely, one indication of vulnerability in the transition process involves coherence between the various military subgroups (perhaps in opposition to a common opponent, civilian rule), acting to coopt and thereby to dominate the fragmented civilian sector. This was certainly the situation in Thailand in mid-1971, as the competing army factions coalesced to dissolve the legislature and constitution and to overturn the transition process.

The Thai experience also suggests a hypothetical pattern for carrying out a successful transition. Once initiated, the process must remain gradual and evolutionary, achieving progress through a series of "participation phases." Although events will occur in a somewhat different sequence and with varying speed in each country, several conceptual phase-lines must be crossed before transition may be considered definitely underway. These phases include:

(1) a second set of national elections;
(2) gradual elimination of appointed members of the legislature;
(3) establishment of provincial branch offices for political parties;
(4) gradual expansion of the political roles of the legislature and other extra-bureaucratic institutions; and
(5) eventual separation of powers and establishment of executive branch accountability.

Once the political system has developed its own set of appropriate mechanisms for holding the executive branch accountable for its performance, it may be credited with having traversed the last phase of a transition from military rule.

It is critical to realize that the military cannot be simply wished away. Politicized army officers accustomed to dominant roles in policy formulation will not remain quietly in their garrisons, at least not for long. Instead, the Thai experience suggests that gradual evolution of a civil-dominant structure requires the country's military leaders to be able to function in the new political environment, and to feel that their role in governing the nation is not threatened with extinction by new civilian decision makers. The military in a transition system remains a major source of political power, whatever those sympathetic to civilian participation and "democracy" might prefer. The military's interests are injected into the decision-making councils of the transition regime; military leaders play a major role in political parties and other extra-bureaucratic institutions. It would no doubt improve the chances of achieving a successful transition if military officers who wanted to deal in national politics had to resign their army positions and to shed their uniforms before doing so. This process was an important element of the relatively successful transition in Turkey, for example, and its absence has hampered institutional development and creation of a viable government political party in Thailand. However, this formal step is less essential than military leaders' perceptions of their possible role in extra-bureaucratic political institutions and their sincere commitment to change. Forcing them to resign from prestigious military positions, though perhaps useful in reducing their coup d'etat organizing power, could provoke an early political crisis, too early, before extra-bureaucratic institutions had the chance to develop and to accrue independent power. In any case, who is in a position to force them to do these things? It seems clear that mechanisms of military participation must exist if the transition process is to lead to long-term restructuring of the political process. If the military is excluded from participation in political decision-making, it will almost certainly take advantage of its formidable experience in coercing its opponents and its high level of organization and discipline to reestablish control.

NOTES

1. Under the leadership of Prime Ministers Khuang Aphaiwong (twice), Thawee Bunyaket, M. R. Seni Pramoj, Pridi Banomyong, and Admiral Luang Thamrong Nawasawat.
2. For the purposes of analysis: November 1974.
3. The latest election is still pending as of the date of this article's preparation: present estimates foresee an election in February 1975.
4. Embodied in Thailand through the so-called Article 17 provisions established by Field Marshal Sarit Thanarat in his 1957 "interim" constitution, empowering the prime minister (Sarit, and subsequently Thanom Kittikachorn) in essence to take whatever harsh measures he deemed necessary in the name of "national security," and overriding any other constitutional or statutory grants of individual rights.
5. In addition to Thanom and Praphat, forced into exile was Colonel Narong Kittikachorn: Thanom's son, Praphat's son-in-law, and a very influential political-military figure prior to the October 1973 revolution.
6. See the *Constitution of the Kingdom of Thailand,* 1968, Official Translation by Kamol Snadhikshetrin, Chief, Legal Technique Division, Office of the Juridical Commission (Bangkok: Thammasat University Press, 1968).
7. Of the 176 members of the appointed Senate in the 1968-1971 period, 103 (59%) were active-duty military officers and another 27 (15%) were civilian officials; none had to resign from these positions to serve in the legislature.
8. These principles appear to be fully compatible with Samuel Huntington's emphasis on institutionalization of non-military structures (*Political Order in Changing Societies,* New Haven, Conn.: Yale University Press, 1968) and with Fred Riggs's focus on balance between various components of the political system (*Administrative Reform and Political Responsiveness: A Theory of Dynamic Balancing,* Beverly Hills, Calif.: Sage Professional Paper in Comparative Politics 01-010, 1970).

DAVID MORELL is a visiting lecturer of politics and government at Princeton University.

Transition from Military Rule

The Case of South Korea

C. I. EUGENE KIM
Western Michigan University

After gaining power through a military coup in May 1961, the Park regime of South Korea has successfully maintained its power until the present. Its longevity is unprecedented in the republican history of South Korea. President Rhee Syngman's First Republic lasted from the 1948 inception of republican government to 1960, when it was overthrown in the wake of massive student uprisings. The Second Republic followed, with Yun Po-son as president and Chang Myon as prime minister. When less than a year old, the Second Republic was overthrown by the military coup headed by then-Major General Park Chung-hee.

This paper is concerned with the nature and development of the Park regime from 1961 to 1975. Since coming into power, how has the Park regime been able to sustain itself? From the May 1961 coup to the creation of Korea's Third Republic in December 1963, the military junta ruled the country. With the creation of the Third Republic, military rulers retired from active service and assumed important political roles as elected and appointed officials. At the same time, significant civilian elements were coopted into the government and the political process.[1] This mixed military-civilian system, however, has resulted neither in greater popular participation in government nor in a peaceful transition of power. It has been able to engineer economic development, but such development has been accompanied by more concentration of power in the hands of President Park, as attested by the 1972 constitutional revision and the creation of Park's Fourth Republic of Korea.[2]

This paper is divided into two main parts. The first explains the factors that contributed to the creation of a mixed military-civilian regime by junta leaders. The second attempts to identify patterns of this mixed military-civilian regime—patterns characterized by Park's greater concentration of power and creation of the Fourth Republic in 1972 through a coup in office.

THE CREATION OF PARK'S MILITARY-CIVILIAN REGIME

One notable aspect of the Korean military coup is that its leaders realized, from the outset of their rule, that they were inadequately qualified to govern the country.[3] Although the coup that brought them into power was almost bloodless, it was planned by a handful of junior officers and had no wide support within the elite military circles.[4] Indeed, there were rumors of countercoups during the critical few days following the initial act. Popular acceptance of the coup was also mixed.[5] Disappointed by the Second Republic's ineffective experiment with democracy, the Korean people accepted the coup as a necessary treatment for the country's deteriorating condition—a treatment announced as only a temporary remedy, not as a permanent cure.[6] An assumption of political sovereignty by the military is alien to Korea's deep-seated Confucian political culture.[7] "Military politics" is regarded with contempt. The coup leaders themselves claimed no superiority and their lowly origins were generally acknowledged. Thus, in pursuit of their goals, they were keenly aware of their limitations and consciously tried to compensate for them.[8]

Once the coup had been achieved, the junta leaders began to consolidate their power. They brought many senior officers into the junta government. They also recruited civilian and academic professionals en masse as advisers and councilors. The Korean CIA was quickly organized as an intelligence agency to counter any antirevolutionary movements. To prove their worth, moreover, the junta leaders instituted many purification and austerity moves. The first Five-Year Plan in the history of the Republic was instituted during the junta period.

For slightly more than two years, the junta government ruled the country with a strong hand. The constitution was abolished; the legislature and political parties were barred. Numerous politicians were purged, blacklisted, and silenced. No demonstrations were permitted. This junta government ended in December 1963, when the Third Republic of Korea was created.

The junta's decision to return the government to civilian hands came early in their assumption of power. In their initial public pledges after the coup, the junta leaders found it expedient to promise reconstitution of a civilian government when their objectives were realized. The forces opposing their continued monopoly of power were too great to ignore. As an obviously unconstitutional, illegitimate assumption of power, the Korean coup could be justified only as a transitional measure for correcting malpractices of the existing civilian regime. And only by thus declaring their government's transitory nature could the junta leaders generate support from the country's powerful armed forces and from the general populace.

The position of the United States in this situation also played a critical role. In planning and executing their action, the coup leaders were careful not to alienate the U.S. government, which has maintained a controlling influence in Korean affairs since the end of World War II. But the first reactions to the coup by U.S. authorities in Korea left the coup leaders in considerable uncertainty. The United Nations Command, U.S. General Carter B. Magruder, and the U.S. Minister in Seoul, Marshall Green, issued two separate statements on the morning of the coup. Both statements supported the overthrown Chang government. The U.S. government was opposed to a military government in Korea. When it was finally forced to recognize the *fait accompli,* it did so reiterating "the strong intent of the military leaders in Korea to return the government to civilian hands."[9]

On August 12, 1961, General Park, as chairman of the junta (Supreme Council for National Reconstruction), announced a timetable for turning the government over to civilian control. A new constitution—the third in the history of the Republic—was to be promulgated by March 1963. A general election would be held in May of that year. The transition was to be completed that summer, and a third Korean republic would then be proclaimed.[10] Only about three months had elapsed from the May coup to Park's announcement, in which the junta leaders affirmed once again the transitional nature of their rule. The purpose of the coup, according to Park, was "to overthrow the antidemocratic system and to lay down the foundation for a true, free democracy in South Korea." In his opinion, the coup was "certainly not for the establishment of a new dictatorship and totalitarianism."[11] Park felt that this definition of the coup's objective was important enough to be repeated often. In another place he stated:

> The military revolution is not the destruction of democracy in Korea. Rather it is a way for saving it; it is a surgical operation intended to exorcise a malignant social, political, and economic tumor. The revolution was staged with the compassion of a benevolent surgeon who sometimes must cause pain in order to preserve life and restore health.[12]

In reconstituting a civilian government, however, the junta leaders had to contend with two tasks of primary importance: (1) revision of the extant constitution and formulation of a new one; and (2) recruitment of a new elite for the third republican government.

The junta leaders envisioned that the new constitution would guarantee the continuation of their measures by a civilian government; but they had no constitutional blueprint.[13] Even the junta's own directive for formulation of a new constitution was vague. According to the August 12 announcement, a new constitution had to be promulgated by March 1963. It would then be submitted to the electorate by a national referendum in fall 1963. Except for designing these preliminary plans, however, the junta leaders pleaded their own ignorance. They were readily assisted by Korean college and university professors and other legal authorities.

A close alliance between coup leaders and intellectuals in legal and social science fields characterized the framing of the third republican constitution. Such an alliance also prevailed in the building of a political party—The Democratic-Republican party (DRP)—as an instrument to recruit personnel into the new civilian government. The idea for this new political party came from J. P. Kim (Kim Chong-p'il), director of the CIA and the number-two man in the junta lineup. However, the detailed plans for the new party were drawn up by several university professors and politicians picked by Kim. One day, according to an informant, Kim approached his secret brain trust with a question which had concerned junta leaders for some time. If civilian rule were restored, what would happen to General Park and others in the junta government? Further, who would man the new civilian government and carry out the junta's programs? The attempt to answer these questions was the effort that culminated in the formation of a new political party—one through which the junta leaders could control the new civilian government.[14]

Several alternatives were apparently considered for the future status of the junta leaders in event of a civilian government's restoration. The junta leaders could all return to barracks, wherein they could still fill the roles of arbiter and kingmaker in the political process—the situation so often manifested in many Latin American countries.[15] Repeated coups remained a possibility. Park, moreover, would be forced to retire soon after his return to garrison duty, although more core junta members were still young field-grade officers. Their return to barracks would mean resumed contention with their superior officers in the Korean military hierarchy. There was yet another alternative: all junta leaders could retire and assume special advisory status within the government, for they wanted a guarantee of privileged status for themselves in a new civilian government. Kim's

TABLE 1
ROK CABINET MINISTERS: YEAR OF BIRTH
(in percentages)

	Aug. '48-April '60	Sept. '60-May '61	Dec. '63-June '71
1900 and before	50.47	19.05	1.35
1901-1910	30.84	38.10	21.62
1911-1920	18.69	42.86	35.14
1921-1930	.0	.0	41.89
1931-1940	.0	.0	.0
Total	100.0%	100.0%	100.0%
(Base)	(107)	(21)	(74)

NOTE: Cases of "no information" are not included in the computation. Totals do not add to 100 due to rounding.
SOURCE: Kim and Lovell data; see note 17.

brain trust, however, was unable to arrive at a suitable solution to these problems about the future of the junta leaders. One alternative remained. This was their assumption of direct political control. The junta leaders could take off their military uniforms and fill important government positions, as either appointed or elected officials. The idea for a new political party thus originated in response to the need for a vehicle by which the junta leaders could assume political power in a new civilian government.[16]

TABLE 2
ROK CABINET MINISTERS: URBAN–RURAL PLACE OF BIRTH
(in percentages)

	Aug. '48-April '60	Sept. '60-May '61	Dec. '63-June '71
Seoul	52.54	26.67	25.53
City over 100,000 (in 1930)	3.39	13.33	8.51
City of 20,000-100,000 (in 1930)	1.69	.0	.0
Rural—all others in Korea	42.37	60.00	65.96
Foreign	.0	.0	.0
Total	100.0%	100.0%	100.0%
(Base)	(59)	(15)	(47)

NOTE: Cases of "no information" are not included in the computation. Totals do not add to 100 due to rounding.
SOURCE: Kim and Lovell data; see note 17.

Within the Third Republic, the Park regime has shown some interesting leadership characteristics. Headed by junta leaders, the regime has also recruited, unlike the regimes of President Rhee and of Premier Chang, large numbers of retired military officers to fill influential government positions. Biographical data about leading personnel and governmental elites in the Park regime, compared with similar data about those of the previous regimes, demonstrate the former's wider representation of different socioeconomic backgrounds.[17]

Generally, the cabinet ministers of the Third Republic are younger and have a wider age distribution than those of the previous regimes. They also come from more rural areas and represent more provinces in the country. In prior occupation, both First Republic and Third Republic elites came from more highly bureaucratic jobs than the elites of the Second Republic. But the bureaucratic work origins of Third Republic cabinet ministers have a much more military aspect than those of the First Republic ministers. The Park regime has shown a very cooptative tendency toward recruiting its governmental leaders; apparently it has been more concerned with the

TABLE 3
ROK CABINET MINISTERS: PRIOR OCCUPATION
(in percentages)

	Aug. '48-April '60	Sept. '60-May '61	Dec. '63-June '71
Central Bureaucracy	31.03	13.73	26.99
Liberal Profession and Professional and Technical[a]	20.00	19.61	16.56
Political Party and/or National Assembly Cabinet Post	11.03	9.80	16.56
Local Gov't. Service	10.34	13.73	8.59
Military	4.83	1.96	19.02
Diplomatic Post	1.38	3.92	3.68
Business	1.38	1.96	1.23
Manager of Public Corp	0.69	0	1.84
Others	0.69	0	0
Total	100.0%	100.0%	100.0%
(Base)	(24)	(40)	(75)

NOTE: Cases of "no information" are not included in the computation. Totals do not add to 100 due to rounding.
a. Liberal profession and professional and technical include college and university professors, educators, lawyers, doctors, journalists, and the like.
SOURCE: Kim and Lovell data; see note 17.

representation of various geographical areas and politically influential groups in the country than with the representation of the people.

The educational backgrounds of Third Republic cabinet ministers are also significant. The Chang cabinet ministers were the most highly educated of the three regimes; all had received at least college- or university-level schooling. About three-fourths of the Rhee cabinet belonged to the highly educated group. For the Park cabinet, the figure is four-fifths. The outstanding feature of the Park cabinet, reflecting in part the technocratic orientation of the regime, is the high proportion of postgraduate education—about one-tenth. Since they are younger than their predecessors, moreover, more of Park's ministers are products of postliberation Korean education; and they are more indigenously oriented and less Western in outlook than previous cabinet ministers.

No Peaceful Exit from Power

The third republican constitution established a limit of two consecutive presidential terms. Perhaps the junta leaders and the framers of their constitution earnestly hoped for a smooth succession to Park and for an eventual peaceful transition of power. The Park regime's development worked against such an eventuality. The constitution, forcefully amended in 1969 to permit Park's candidacy for a third term in 1971, was totally discarded in 1972 for a new constitution—this one to legitimize Park's lifetime presidency. What actually happened in 1972 was a coup in office; and Park thus succeeded in creating a fourth republic in South Korea.

Though personally introspective, rustic in appearance, and short of temper, Park had a clean reputation as a general.[18] His professional devotion to his military career was well marked and respected by his junior officers.[19] In 1963, he was not even certain whether he should run for president as urged by his followers.[20] Park's political stature, however, has grown during his tenure in office. His influence, particularly in the eyes of his followers, has been politically stabilizing. His regime's determination and direction have resulted in an impressive rate of economic growth, contributing to the improvement of the country's international standing.[21]

Under Park's administration, the number of countries with which South Korea has established diplomatic relations has increased significantly. In early 1975 South Korea maintains cultural and economic ties with many nations. Park has also traveled widely in the United States, Australia, Germany, and countries of southeast Asia. Seoul, the capital city, has been host to numerous international conferences with participants from many

TABLE 4
ROK CABINET MINISTERS: LEVEL OF CIVILIAN EDUCATION
(in percentages)

	Aug. '48-April '60	Sept. '60-May '61	Dec. '63- June '71
Primary or less	1.0	0.0	0.0
Secondary	23.3	0.0	16.2
College or University	72.8	95.2	71.6
Postgraduate	2.9	4.8	12.2
Total	100.0%	100.0%	100.0%
(Base)	(103)	(21)	(74)

NOTE: The cases of "no information" are not included in the computation.
SOURCE: Kim and Lovell data; see note 17.

countries. Also, for the first time in Korea's recorded history, Koreans have voluntarily fought outside the immediate areas of their peninsula; they have shown much pride in the ability of their troops in Vietnam.[22] Among the economic achievements of the Park regime has been the institution of successful five year plans. Beginning in 1962, both the first and second of these—regarded as too ambitious by outside observers—were successfully implemented. The GNP increased at an average annual growth rate of more than 8% in the planned period. Private consumption expenditure almost doubled to 970 billion *won* from 1962 to 1970. Per capita income also doubled, to about 200 U.S. dollars, by 1970. Exports began to rise, amounting to 658.3 million U.S. dollars in 1969—more than ten times the 1962 figure.[23]

Under Park, "productive administration" has been emphasized. Political nicety has been put aside. "Less politics" is regarded as more conducive to administrative and economic development.[24] Park has also concentrated the power of his presidential secretariat and cabinet in the hands of technocrats, not party politicians.[25]

The duty of the technocrats is to serve, not to provide political leadership or to compete with Park for power. Park's posture of "less politics" has also helped to undermine the political viability of his party (DRP). The DRP is an instrument good enough to use for electoral mobilization, but it no longer functions for purposes of policy input. Under Park's leadership, the DRP has failed to develop as an active agent for personnel recruitment and policy-making. Forced to play a secondary role, the DRP has thus suffered from internal dissent and factional squabbling. As I have stated elsewhere, "If political development involves the cultivation of a meaningful interplay of various interests and the development of a political party as an agent aggregating such interests for policy making, Park has not helped such development. On the contrary, Park's achievements have been at the expense of the DRP's development as a viable political institution."[26]

At the time the 1969 constitutional amendments were made, the two main factions within the DRP were the so-called mainstream and anti-mainstream factions.[27] The mainstream faction was headed by J. P. Kim, and associated with it were most core members of the 1961 coup. Its ultimate objective was to run Kim for president when Park's second term expired in 1971. The anti-mainstream's objective was to block Kim's presidency. This faction consisted of anti-Kim junta members plus numerous civilian politicians and assemblymen who had been coopted into the party. Park's role was to maintain balance between the two factions.[28] Apparently Park, at least in the beginning, wanted to remain non-committal on the issue of his third term.[29] Eventually, however, he sided with the anti-mainstream faction and approved the 1969 constitutional amendments. The question was, could the DRP survive the possible succession crisis if Park completed his second term and retired, even temporarily, from politics? Anti-mainstream forces argued that only Park could provide the strong leadership required to maintain political stability and to continue South Korea's rapid economic development.[30] Their reasoning was also based on factors of national security. Transfer of power, they maintained, would entail political unrest that could well be exploited by North Korean subversive provocations.[31]

In 1971, Park was reelected to a third term. His followers asked then the question they had previously asked: "What will happen to President Park and to us if Park should retire from politics?" The worst could be expected. The Park regime has oppressed its opposition, and the CIA has become an awesome instrument for silencing dissidents. There were rumors that Park's administration and the DRP intended eventually to make Park lifetime president. One of the major campaign issues against Park and his DRP in 1971 was their continued stay in power, and the opposition NDP (New Democratic party) made an impressive showing. In the National Assembly election, particularly, NDP candidates won more seats than party strategists had predicted.

Park was elected president in 1963 and 1967 with 46.7% and 51.4% respectively of valid votes cast. In 1971, Park's winning margin was 53.2%—his best showing in the three elections.[32] In the National Assembly, the DRP won 110 and 130 seats of a total of 175 in 1963 and 1967, and only 113 seats of a total of 204 in 1971. DRP candidates received 32.4%, 52.8%, and 47.7% of total valid votes cast in 1963, 1967, and 1971.

These statistics show a steady increase in Park's electoral strength. In the DRP, however, electoral strength for the National Assembly election peaked in 1967, then declined significantly in 1971. The causes of this decline were many. Essentially, the NDP's campaign against the DRP's two-thirds majority in the National Assembly had proved effective. Popular opposition to another constitutional amendment through the DRP-controlled National Assembly was apparent.

To DRP strategists, Park has become an electoral necessity for maintaining themselves in power. Without Park, they have become uncertain of preserving their status through electoral means. If Park should retire from politics, the DRP must be assured that he would be followed by a personally chosen successor. In 1971, NDP opposition was too strong for such a guarantee to be made.

During the 1971 election, Park reflected that his presidency had been a heavy burden on him. He is reported to have said, "I think I shall not run any more after this."[33] When Park was inaugurated on July 1 in his third term, however, "Korean political observers were struck by the absence of any suggestion in Park's inaugural speech that his third term would be his last."[34] The opposition speculated that the DRP would attempt to change the constitution again in 1974; and that once Park had been made lifetime president, South Korea would hold no more elections.[35] What sped this timetable and dictated how the new Fourth Constitution was drawn and implemented were rapid changes in the international scene—events that deeply affected the security perception of Park and his government. Among these events were President Nixon's Guam Declaration of 1969; the U.S. intention to reduce its military presence in Asia; Peking's admission to the UN; the visits to Peking of Nixon and Japanese Premier Tanaka; the subsequent establishment of formal diplomatic ties between Japan and mainland China; and North Korea's growing diplomatic offensive. South Korea's reaction to these changes was to tighten internal security and to move toward an understanding with North Korea. Finally, progress on both these fronts strengthened Park's hand and facilitated his clever coup in office, the creation of the Fourth Republic.[36]

As a prelude to creation of the Fourth Republic and in an attempt to deal with the international developments surrounding Korea, a national emergency decree was activated on December 6, 1971. According to Park, the decree was necessary to cope with the changes in the international situation and to meet North Korea's "aggressive design."[37] The DRP-controlled Assembly, without the participation of opposition party members, passed a bill on December 26 that gave Park extraordinary emergency powers. The dramatic North-South Joint Communique for peaceful reunification of the country through negotiation was announced on July 4, 1972. Martial law was subsequently declared on October 17. In the martial law declaration, Park stated that "The Extraordinary State Council shall announce by October 27, 1972 the draft amendments to the present Constitution with the view of peaceful unification of the nation."[38]

THE FOURTH REPUBLIC

An outstanding feature of the Fourth Constitution of the Republic of Korea is the distinction and emphasis it gives to the office of president. In fact, the structure of the entire Fourth Republic is based on the changes established in that office and in its relationship to the other branches of government.

Comparing the two constitutions item by item, we see that there were almost no changes in the provisions dealing with courts, election management, local self-government, and the economy.[39] The chapter on "Rights and Duties of Citizens" in the Fourth Constitution, however, shows significant modification from the Third Constitution in areas of freedom of speech, press, assembly, association, collective bargaining, and action by workers. The democratic principles involved have become restricted by liberal use of the modifying clause, "provided by law."

Missing in the Fourth Constitution, moreover, is an effort to encourage the institutional growth of political parties. In the Fourth Constitution, as in the Third Constitution, a plural party system is guaranteed—but now candidates for elective office no longer need gain the endorsement of duly recognized political parties. Candidates for the presidency and the National Assembly may run as independents—the very practice that Park and other leaders of the 1961 coup had feared—and attempted to correct—as a source of irresponsible politicians and politicking. Park is now placed above politics and political parties. The Fourth Constitution even denies that political parties are necessary.

The National Conference for Unification is a notable new addition to the Fourth Constitution. Defined as "a national organization based on the collective will of the people as a whole to pursue peaceful unification of the fatherland" (Art. 35), it is charged with the election of the president. But, as previously stated, it must function strictly as a nonpartisan body, and candidates are barred from membership in political parties (Art. 37, Sec. 3). It is, moreover, a huge body—to be composed of not fewer than

2,000 or more than 5,000 members (for the first National Conference, elected on December 15, 1972, the size was set at 2,359 members). Members are directly elected by voters for a three-year term, and the president of the republic serves as chairman. The National Conference's other functions include: (1) approving a list of one-third of all National Assembly members to be appointed by the president for a three-year term (other members of the National Assembly are directly elected by voters for a six-year term); and (2) approving all constitutional amendments proposed to it by the National Assembly.

In the transition from the Third Constitution to the Fourth Constitution, Park, as incumbent president, assumed chairmanship of the newly elected National Conference and was elected first president of the Fourth Republic on December 23, 1972. His term of office is now fixed at six years, in contrast to his previous four year limit; but his tenure is now constitutionally unrestricted (the Third Constitution, as amended in 1969, had limited him to three consecutive terms).

As chairman of the National Conference and as president of the Fourth Republic of Korea, Park has placed himself above the regular branches of government. Electorally, he is responsible only to the National Conference, and his extensive powers are now virtually unchecked. The structures of the one-house National Assembly and the Supreme Court are much weaker in the Fourth Republic than in its predecessor. As for local self-government, the Fourth Constitution states specifically that "Local assemblies under the present Constitution shall not be formed until the unification of the fatherland has been achieved" (Supplementary Art. 10).

CONCLUSION

Park's mixed military-civilian regime has displayed an impressive rate of economic and social development and modernization. It has also manifested, however, an increasingly centralistic, authoritarian tendency. And it has forcefully amended its original 1963 constitution, in 1969 and again in 1972, finally legitimizing a lifetime presidency for Park. As Bienen and Morell maintain, if transition from military rule entails political decentralization, a limited resort to coercion, and a peaceful transfer of power, the Park regime has taken a reverse course of development.[40] Such a reverse trend, exemplified by South Korea, has resulted from: (1) the low level of Korean political culture, as shown by the extent of political instability and the lack of legitimacy; (2) the personalized notion of politics and the high-risk factors associated with the game of politics; and (3) the international situation surrounding the Korean peninsula, which creates an aura of legitimacy for Park's desire for continued power.

The Park regime has perceived the problem of nation building as a mission—its sole responsibility and charge. Any tangible sign of achievement is self-fulfilling proof of its righteousness; and the Park regime tends to feel itself indispensable to Korea's continued growth and development. The opposition party is perceived as disorganized, incapable of governing, and divisive of national unity.[41]

Another critical reason for the Park regime's authoritarian direction is that it believes that any transfer of power would be very risky. As the coup was an illegitimate act at the outset, a question nagging the coup leaders has concerned their own uncertain status if they relinquish their power. Factional struggle within the leadership, moreover, has vitiated any possible original constructive intention of institutionalizing political succession.

With the creation of the Fourth Republic, Park has placed himself above politics and has concentrated much more in his own hands. The facility with which this transition was accomplished can be attributed to changes in the international scene affecting the security perception of the Korean people. As stated by Park, moreover, the Fourth Republic is to prepare the nation for negotiation with North Korea toward the desired peaceful reunification of the Korean peninsula.

NOTES

1. Henry Bienen and David Morell, "Transition from Military Rule: Thailand and Nigeria," paper presented at the Inter-University Seminar on Armed Forces and Society, October 11-13, 1973, p. 1.

2. For some relevant works, see Edward Feit, ed., *The Armed Bureaucrats* (Boston: Houghton Mifflin Co., 1973); Morris Janowitz, *The Military in the Political Development of New Nations* (Chicago: University of Chicago Press, Phoenix Books, 1964); and Samuel P. Huntington, *Political Order in Changing Societies* (New Haven: Yale University Press, 1968), ch. 4.

3. Morris Janowitz has made a similar observation. See his *The Military in the Political Development of New Nations*, p. 92.

4. For an official history of the coup, see (ROK) Kunsa Hyongmyong-sa P'yonch'an Wiwon-hoe (Committee for the Compilation of the Korean Military Revolution), *Kunsa Hyongmyong-sa* [History of the Military Revolution] (Seoul, 1963), 2 vols. Hereafter cited as *Kunsa Hyongmyong-sa* [History of the Military Revolution].

5. *New York Times*, May 28, 1961.

6. For recent, scholarly books on the Second Republic, see Sungjoo Han, *The Failure of Democracy in South Korea* (Berkeley: University of California Press, 1974); Se-jin Kim, *The Politics of Military Revolution in Korea* (Chapel Hill: University of North Carolina Press, 1971); John K.C. Oh, *Korea: Democracy on Trial* (Ithaca: Cornell University Press, 1968); and Gregory Henderson, *Korea: The Politics of the Vortex* (Cambridge: Harvard University Press, 1968).

7. Henderson, p. 17. See also Pyong-choon Hahm, *The Korean Political Tradition and Law* (Seoul: Hollym Corporation, 1967), ch. 1.

8. C. I. Eugene Kim, "The South Korean Military Coup of May, 1961: Its Causes and the Social Characteristics of Its Leaders," in Jacques Van Doorn, ed., *Armed Forces and Society* (The Hague: Mouton, 1968), pp. 298-316.

9. United Press International, Washington, D.C., May 19, 1961. See also John K.C. Oh, "Role of the United States in South Korea's Democratization," *Pacific Affairs* 43, 2 (Summer 1969): 164-177.

10. *Kunsa Hyongmyong-sa* [History of the Military Revolution], p. 236.

11. Park Chung Hee, *Chido ja-do* [The Ways of a Leader] (Seoul: SCNR, 1961), pp. 23-25.

12. Park Chung Hee, *Uri Minjok ui Nagal Kil* [Our Nation's Path] (Seoul: Tong a Ch'ulp'an-sa, 1961), pp. 197-198.

13. A statement to this effect was issued by Colonel Yi Sok-che and General Yi Chu-il. See (ROK) National Assembly, *Honbop Kejong Sinui-rok* [Verbatim Reports of the Consultative Proceedings on Constitutional Amendments] (Seoul, 1967), Vol. 1, pp. 504-505 and Vol. 2, pp. 7-9 respectively. Hereafter cited as *The 3rd Republic Constitutional Consultative Proceedings*.

14. This information was derived from the author's interview with an informant who was a member of J. P. Kim's brain trust. The interview was conducted in summer 1969.

15. S. E. Finer, *The Man on Horseback* (New York: Praeger, 1962), pp. 151 ff., 168.

16. Jae Souk Sohn, "Political Dominance and Political Failure: The Role of the Military in the Republic of Korea," in Henry Bienen, ed., *The Military Intervenes* (New York: Russell Sage Foundation, 1968), pp. 115-116. Professor Sohn argues that the military revolutionaries were reluctant from the outset to transfer the government to civilian control.

17. The data here are drawn from the author's study in progress jointly with John P. Lovell on *The Social Background Data on the Government Elites of the Republic of Korea, 1948-1972*. The grants from the Social Science Research Council and Western Michigan University in 1973 for the analysis of the data are gratefully acknowledged. In this paper, only the socioeconomic backgrounds of cabinet ministers are analyzed. See also Bae-ho Hahn and Kyu-taik Kim, "Korean Political Leaders (1952-1962): Their Social Origins and Skills," Asian Survey 2, 7 (July 1963): 305-323.

18. Interview with a former colleague of President Park.

19. Chong-shim Kim, *Seven Years with Korea's Park Chung-hee* (Seoul: Hollym Corporation, 1967), passim.

20. C. I. Eugene Kim, "Significance of the 1963 Korean Elections," Asian Survey 4, 3 (March 1964): 765-773.

21. Princeton Lyman, "Korea's Involvement in Vietnam," Orbis 12, 2 (Summer 1968): 568-581. See also David Steinberg, *Korea: Nexus of East Asia* (New York: American-Asian Educational Exchange, Inc., 1968), p. 22. See also for an analysis of interplay of politics and economics, David C. Cole and Princeton N. Lyman, *Korean Development: The Interplay of Politics and Economics* (Cambridge: Harvard University Press, 1971).

22. Lyman, op. cit.

23. P. W. Kuznets, "The Korean Take-off," paper presented at the 1971 annual meeting of the Association for Asian Studies. See also Mahn Je Kim (President of

Korea Development Institute), "A Decade and Future Perspectives of the Korean Economic Development," prepared for presentation to the Symposium on "Korea and the Powers in the 1970's," sponsored by the Institute for Asian Studies, Washington, D.C., April 20-21, 1973. See also for various economic problems associated with rapid economic growth, Kae H. Chung, "Industrial Progress in South Korea," Asian Survey 14, 5 (May 1974): 439-455.

24. Joung-sik Lee, "The Prospects of Korean Politics in the 1970s," Koreana Quarterly 13, 1-2 (Spring-Summer 1970): 1-17.

25. C. I. Eugene Kim, "Institution-Building and Adaptation: The Case of the DRP in South Korea," paper presented at the 1972 annual meeting of the American Political Science Association, September 5-9, 1972. See also Sang-ki Paik, "A Study of Decision-making Process in the Chungwadae," Koreana Quarterly 2, 2 (Summer 1969): 35-58.

26. C. I. Eugene Kim, "The Meaning of the 1971 Korean Elections; A Pattern of Political Development," Asian Survey 12, 3 (March 1972): 224. See also Yong-bok Ko, "Political Parties and Factionalism in Korea," Koreana Quarterly 9, 2 (Summer 1967): 18-37.

27. Y. C. Han, "Political Parties and Political Development in South Korea," Pacific Affairs 17, 4 (Winter 1969-1970): 446-464; and "The 1969 Constitutional Revision and Party Politics in South Korea," Pacific Affairs 44, 2 (Summer 1971): 242-258. See also Kwan Bong Kim, *The Korea-Japan Treaty Crisis and the Instability of the Korean Political System* (New York: Praeger, 1971), pp. 202 ff.

28. Y. C. Han, "Political Parties and Political Development in South Korea," p. 464.

29. Dong-a Ilbo, July 8, 1969.

30. Y. C. Han, "Political Parties and Political Development in South Korea," pp. 459-460.

31. Ibid.

32. C. I. Eugene Kim, "The Meaning of the 1971 Elections in Korea: A Pattern of Political Development," pp. 213-224. See Jae-on Kim and B. C. Koh, "Electoral Behavior and Social Development in South Korea: An Aggregate Data Analysis of Presidential Elections," Journal of Politics 34, 2 (August 1972): 825-859.

33. Quoted in Korea Week, April 30, 1971.

34. Ibid., July 15, 1971.

35. Ibid., May 15, 1971.

36. C. I. Eugene Kim, "Korea at the Crossroads: The Birth of the Fourth Republic," Pacific Affairs 46, 2 (Summer 1973): 218-231.

37. Ibid.

38. See Han K. Kim, ed., *Reunification of Korea: 50 Basic Documents* (Washington, D.C.: Institute for Asian Studies, 1972).

39. C. I. Eugene Kim, "Korea at the Crossroads: The Birth of the Fourth Republic," pp. 218-231.

40. Bienen and Morell, as cited in note 1 of this paper.

41. Young Whan Kihl, "Leadership and Opposition Role Perception among Party Elites," Korea Journal (September 1973): 4-23.

C. I. EUGENE KIM is a professor of political science at Western Michigan University, and is the editor of the recent volume entitled Korean Unification: Problems and Prospects.

Civilianization of Military Regimes in the Arab World

GABRIEL BEN-DOR
University of Haifa

One who studies modern Arab political history studies, by necessity, the role of the military in Arab politics. In 7 Arab countries, between 1939 and 1969, 41 coups were attempted by the military; 23 were successful.[1] In most key Arab countries (Egypt, Syria, Algeria, Iraq, Sudan, Libya) there have been coups resulting in the establishment of military regimes. In several others, the military constitute the backbone of the regime (Jordan), arbitrate in civil wars (Lebanon), or constantly threaten actual or potential coups (Morocco). Thus, by far the most important single factor in Arab politics is the army; by far the most important type of regime is military.

A great deal of scholarly attention has been paid to the causes, patterns, and outcomes of military intervention in Arab politics.[2] Among other things, we can cite the continuity of direct or indirect military rule in Islamic history, the existence of the military as a corporate interest group, as the vanguard of the new (salaried) or "old" middle class, as the most modern-oriented group in society, as the breaker of political stalemates, or as the epitomizers of praetorian power in weakly institutionalized societies as the major explanations for military intervention in Arab politics.[3] There are also good case studies (with notable exceptions, mostly descriptive rather than theoretically oriented) of military regimes and politicians. Our understanding of the dynamics of the behavior of the Arab military in politics, therefore, on the whole rests on fairly well-established grounds.

In contrast, it is almost impossible to find research on the gradual or sudden disengagement of the military from direct rule.[4] Although rare, such sudden withdrawals have occurred fairly recently in the Arab world

(Syria, 1954 and 1961; Sudan, 1964) and elsewhere in the Middle East (Turkey, 1961 and 1971). Gradual and partial civilianization of Arab military regimes, as will be shortly demonstrated, is most certainly in evidence. One of the most significant questions of Middle East politics is the possibility of civilianizing Arab military regimes.

Armies may have intervened to protect their own interests, yet, when they have done so, at what point will they feel that these interests are secured to the extent that withdrawal from direct rule is possible and desirable? It is difficult to conceive of such a point. They may have moved in with the limited aim of removing a certain regime; however, such removal may open so many wounds, may cause so many splits and cleavages, and may create so much enmity and so many threats that the officers may consider withdrawal much too dangerous and in fact impossible.[5] They may have been motivated by goals of reform and modernization; however, can we imagine any army claiming that, "modernization" having been "accomplished," it is time to return to the barracks?

One's goals may change once one has obtained power: ambitions may grow; power may become a goal in its own right. Ruling becomes an agreeable habit. The fear looms that others will act in vengeance once one is out of power. Thus, just as military intervention has its own dynamics, so does military disengagement. To a certain extent each must be studied on its own. The investigator must realize that theoretical research about them does not necessarily relate to the same clusters of variables.

ABRUPT VERSUS GRADUAL TRANSITION

If we use two major variables (the level of the institutionalization of the polity and the rate of disengagement), a simplified typology emerges (see Figure 1).

	Relatively High	Relatively Low		
	a Mexico	c Egypt	Gradual, partial civilianizing	Rate of Withdrawal
	b Turkey	d Ghana	Abrupt change of government	

Figure 1: **LEVEL OF INSTITUTIONALIZATION**[6]

In the Arab world, we find mostly types "c" and "d."[7] In general, the majority of scholars agree that Arab politics are characterized by what Vatikiotis calls weak institutions and the lack of a strong sense of community.[8] Thus, Mexico and Turkey, where the struggle is between the military, on the one hand, and a fairly well-institutionalized party structure (which the military may have helped to create), on the other—all within a fairly strongly established political community—are models almost totally inapplicable to the Arab cases. Inasmuch as each of the four models is characterized by its own political dynamics, we shall concentrate on types "c" and "d." According to the contention of this paper, "c" is the most important and most probable pattern of civilianizing political regimes in the Arab world.

The abrupt withdrawals have proved to be distinctly temporary (Sudan, withdrawal in 1964, reintervention in 1969; Syria, withdrawal in 1954, reintervention in 1957-1958, withdrawal again in 1961, and reintervention in 1962, reestablishing a military regime). Another Middle Eastern example is Turkey. Elsewhere in the so-called developing world we find numerous other examples (Ghana, Burma, Argentina, and so on) of abrupt withdrawals by armies, then short periods of civilian rule, followed by the reentry of the military to a dominant role in political life. Obviously, military disengagement as such is a rather infrequent, complicated, and difficult process. The abruptness of sudden withdrawal is probably caused by factors which are temporary and transitory.

A preliminary analysis indicates a few convincing explanations of the temporary character of abrupt withdrawals. All Arab cases followed large-scale, unique political upheavals. In Sudan, there were massive popular dissatisfaction, unrest, protest, demonstrations, and strikes. In Syria, a five-year military dictatorship was overthrown by a heterogeneous, uneasy coalition of forces (1954). The most serious attempt to bring about Arab unity failed with the dissolution of the United Arab Republic (the Egyptian-Syrian union) in 1961.

The armies of the countries involved were considerably affected by these events. There were hesitations, stemming from doubts about the legitimacy of military rule. There was a decline in the military's self-confidence, both because of the series of developments and because of the general uncertainty following major political upheavals. In addition, the uneasiness of the coalitions effecting these political changes was reflected within the officer corps. The uneasiness undermined their unity and capacity for taking unified, cohesive political action, at least for a short period. (Eventually this led, in at least two of the countries, to precisely the type of factionalism which motivates the military to stage coups.) There was, then, a momentary, partial political paralysis. A number of related factors could be observed—the perception of the existence of alternative political forces, the impact of the shortcomings and failures of the previous political performance of the military, and the attempts to reestablish a more favorable political image of the military, both within and outside the army.

Civilian rule in all three cases was short-lived, because the upheavals had a superficial impact. It was superficial because it failed to undermine the dominant political potential of the military and to create and to strengthen an institutionalized capability for civilian groups. These groups could neither contain and curtail the strength of the military nor persuade the officers to accept a civilian framework of politics in which they could participate either as individual politicians or as an organized pressure group—but *not* as a corporate faction oriented to the center of political power via the use or threat of force. A more important, permanent, and significant (and, of course, far more limited in extent) pattern of civilianizing is the gradual model.

INCREASING REGIME STABILITY

Gradual civilianization is a recent phenomenon in the Arab world. It was born in the 1960s and is far more clearly apparent in the 1970s. The wave of military coups flooding the Arab Middle East since 1949 more or less had come to an end by 1969. Since then, hardly a major coup has taken place—the exceptions are the bloodless coup in Syria in 1970 and the bloody coup in Sudan in 1971. There is a new stability in the military regimes, notwithstanding the dire predictions of some analysts just a few years ago. In Egypt since 1954 or 1970 (Sadat's accession upon Nasser's death), in Algeria since 1965, in Sudan and Libya since 1969, in Syria since 1963 (the *Baath*-oriented military regime came to power in 1963 and experienced a violent, successful coup in 1966 and a bloodless one in 1970), in Iraq since 1968, there have been by comparative standards appropriate to the region, relatively long periods of uninterrupted rule by a group of men or by a junta dominated by a single leader.

This stability survived, in Egypt and Syria, both major defeat on the battlefield (in 1967) and relative success in war (in 1973). It is obviously related to the end of the Arab cold war in the 1950s and 1960s. This cold war,[9] waged along personal and regime-oriented lines and couched in highly ideological, emotion-laden political language, presented the Arab world as a most intricate political system. The duality of independent Arab states and the unchallenged, ubiquitously quoted ideal of Arab unity brought about the existence of eighteen Arab polities. They proved to be extremely vulnerable to external (that is, inter-Arab) incitement, manipulation, subversion, and other forms of intervention. The inter-Arab cold war was waged along various cleavages. At one time it was between the military, so-called progressive and socialist regimes, on the one hand, and the so-called feudal monarchies, on the other. At other times, the issue was between the Nasserist and Syrian or Iraqi (*Baath*ist and other) versions of Arab unity and the leadership of the Arab world. As long as this cold war went on, there was a constant attrition of energy, and a constant uphill battle to fight the danger to the legitimacy, and at times to the physical existence and survival, of military regimes. With the decline and near-termination of the Arab cold war—which came about when the implementation or Arab unity was postponed to the distant future, the ideological tension of the Messianic component of the ideal of Arab unity declined, and a more inward-looking political orientation arose—one major threat to the stability of military regimes has almost disappeared.

Another factor contributing to increasing stability is simply the immense concentration of sheer coercive power in the hands of the ruling officers. The power of power ought not to be ignored. With time, the military rulers have mastered and improved what may be conveniently termed "governmental technology," which includes administration, centralized and shrewd distribution of resources and propaganda, and the utilization of widespread and often ruthless security measures. Once this technology, based on the coercive power of the regime, reaches a certain level of sophistication, the chances of the regime's remaining in power increase very considerably indeed.

Partly as a result of these factors, opposition to the Arab military regimes has declined to the point where, in some cases, it has virtually vanished. The end of the cold war has deprived it of external support, the massive coercive power of the regime has destroyed potential bases of support at home, and never-ending factional struggle has destroyed it physically and morally. The rulers' attempts to eliminate all actual or potential centers of alternative power have been rather successful. Once the civilian opposition was more or less eliminated, it was easier to stifle and to destroy opposition within the army. Deprived of civilian allies and catalysts, weakened by the long series of internal struggles and coups, military opposition has by and large been defeated or reduced to virtual inactivity.

Under such circumstances, the self-confidence of the military regimes significantly increased (while that of the potential opposition drastically declined). It became possible to devote time and energy to dealing with external and internal problems. In Syria, this involved a fairly radical attempt to transform society in the direction of the socialist ideals of the *Baath*. In Egypt, as well as in Syria, it involved a greatly enhanced capacity to confront the military might and to undermine the diplomatic position of Israel.[10] The relative success of these attempts (especially the latter) further enhanced the prestige, self-confidence, and power of the Arab regimes.

It is against this background that gradual civilianization must be analyzed. In Egypt, the Arab country which has enjoyed the longest period of stability, gradual civilianization is evident in the composition of the highest political echelons. As Beeri points out,[11] in 1954, 18 of the top 27 men in power were officers (including the 11 uniformed members of the all-important Revolutionary Command Council and 7 of the 16 members of the government, among whom the officers held all the highest posts). In 1964, among the top 39 Egyptian leaders, Beeri found only 14 officers, although they still held the key posts.[12] Nevertheless, their numbers declined, they no longer wore uniforms, they attempted to legitimize their rule through elections, and they began to rely heavily on civilian experts, technocrats, and bureaucrats. In 1974, only the president-prime minister (Sadat), one vice-president, one deputy prime minister, and two ministers were officers, out of three deputy prime ministers and thirty ministers.[13] The number of civilians in centers of political power (and not just as experts to be consulted, but as meaningful participants in political decision-making) has been constantly increasing in Egypt.

The case of Syria has been called by one scholar "the army-party symbiosis."[14] The military regime in power since 1963 has indeed maintained a close working relationship with the socialist-nationalist *Baath* party. The *Baath*, perhaps the most articulate party in the Arab world ideologically, has—and again, this may be a "first" or at least a "most" among Arab political parties—branches in several other countries and has enjoyed a relationship with the ruling Iraqi military somewhat similar to its relationship with the military regime in power in Syria. The *Baath* has been split into numerous factions and subfactions. In and of itself, it has been unable to come anywhere near getting into power. Its performance in relatively free elections has been rather poor. It has not had much success, under nonmilitary rule, in building institutional strength (we are discussing poorly institutionalized political systems in general). It has been plagued by fratricidal extreme factionalism. Nevertheless, the *Baath* has been a most useful and convenient political civilian partner to Syria's military rulers.

The *Baath* has supplied the ideology and, to a large extent, the legitimization of the regime. It has been used to create links with segments of the intelligentsia, students, and youth. It has supplied the political model and the organizational framework for mobilizing peasants, workers, students, and soldiers. In the once seemingly unceasing series of coups and countercoups of the 1960s, the various military factions more or less neutralized and at times simply destroyed one another. The remaining factions have been lacking in political cadres of their own. Political cadres are needed both to organize civilian support for the regime and to help with the political mobilization necessary for the ambitious reforms the regime desires. Moreover, the ideological and organizational skills of the *Baath* cadres have been used to create a tight network of control and foci of identification with the regime *within* the Syrian army.[15] Thus, in Syria, the military has achieved what its counterpart in Egypt failed to accomplish for so long—fairly large-scale mass mobilization through a political party closely tied to the army that yet appears to have some meaningful existence in its own right.

EGYPT AND SYRIA COMPARED

In both Egypt and Syria, ultimate power still seems to lie with the military. The genesis of their regimes was clearly military—army officers captured power through the use or threat of force, replaced incumbents, and eliminated rivals through (at times, massive) coercion. They raised military men (in the beginning in uniform) to the top, manned almost all key posts and centers of decision-making with officers or ex-officers, and put all other centers of power under tight control. As we have just seen, this initial picture of outright military dictatorship is no longer accurate. However, it is certain that, if any serious or open challenge to the regime were made, the military would act successfully to quell it and to ensure its own ultimate dominance in politics. Although civilian politicians in Egypt and party functionaries in Syria are gaining in political power, it would be impossible for them to continue to rule if the support of the military were withdrawn. The technocrat-politicians of Egypt, who by and large lack organized partisan bases, and the *Baath* functionaries in Syria, have been given a share of power by the military. But they could neither hold that share against the will of the military, nor utilize it successfully against the military.[16]

What they can do is deepen their penetration into the top echelons of politics while refraining from challenging the military. In any case, past experience with attempts to do the contrary has been very unhappy. The military wing of the *Baath* has always won out over the various civilian wings; and the Egyptian regime has already won out over the various civilian wings; and the Egyptian regime has already gone as far as, on two occasions, disbanding political parties of its own creation. In this sense, civilianization has been not only gradual, but also rather partial. As the original members of the Free Officers in Egypt, for instance, disappear from the political arena (by 1974, only two of its original members, Sadat and Shafei, still held central political posts), the civilian component of this military-civil partnership may grow even stronger. If inter-Arab tensions remain low,[17] opposition is weak, the regime's self-confidence grows, and the original members of the military junta die out, eventually the Egyptian political system may well evolve along lines similar to those of Turkey. This, in effect, means that the military will be the ultimate veto group playing the role of watchdog over the rules of the game. However, under normal circumstances, it will let the civilians govern, staging only occasional veto coups, and signaling from time to time the bounds within which civilian politicians must stay.[18]

Similarly, it is also possible that, in Syria, the *Baath* party will have an increasingly important role in political life—again, within bounds defined ultimately by the military. The party may deepen its penetration into the army, and the partisan component of the "army-party symbiosis" may eventually supply the majority of politicians in the top posts in the country.[19] If the level of institutionalization rises considerably in the Arab countries (and this is very much an open question, although it seems safe to state that in all probability it is rising and will rise in the future to some extent), passing a certain threshold, the Egyptian model may eventually resemble Turkey in the 1960s and 1970s (strong, competitive party system and military veto group). The Syrian model may resemble Turkey under Ataturk (increasingly strong single party used by the military to carry out a long series of social reforms initiated by the leaders of the army).[20]

ARAB PATTERNS

Notwithstanding significant differences in the political history and social structure of the various Arab countries, in general the Egyptian and Syrian models are applicable all over the Arab world. Facing weak political communities in lowly institutionalized polities, most Arab countries have opted for solving the problem by attempting to build a Western type of nation-state,[21] based on a military-dominated, strong, power-oriented political center. This center uses both massive coercive power and a new set of social and national symbols embodied in civilian political mechanisms to bring the large periphery into the framework of the nation-state. To the extent that civilianization can be expected to occur in the Arab nations, it will occur in all probability along the lines of the two models presented here or in some sort of fusion between them.[22]

The social scientist must face disappointment when considering the implications of the analysis. Thus far, the impact of outside powers on civilianization in the Arab world has been almost nonexistent. Military regimes gain international recognition very easily—a factor which tends to increase the temptation for the potential coup-makers. International recognition and aid (both military and economic) have not been contingent, as a rule, on the character of the given regime. The great powers apparently have neither the wish nor the capacity to use their influence to transform others' internal regimes. They know that, if pressured, a given Arab regime almost always has the option of orienting itself to a competing foreign power. They also realize that, while bringing down a weak regime may not be too difficult, it may be impossible to help build anything more durable that may be of some use to the given outside power.

Outside military aid to the Arab military regimes has come largely from the Soviet Union[23] (to Egypt, Syria, Iraq, Algeria, and Yemen), which on the whole has shown no sign of being unhappy with military regimes. Indeed, at times it has described military regimes as "progressive" manifestations of the stage of the "national bourgeoisie" liberating its country and opening new possibilities of social progress. In any case, all foreign military aid has been channeled through the military, thus contributing nothing to the strengthening of civilian groups or institutions. In a later stage of stronger institutionalization, a different outcome is possible; but for the time being, military aid has had almost no impact on civilianization.[24]

The greatest contribution of the outside world to civilianization has been the little it did to help create stability both in inter-Arab relations and within the various Arab countries. As we have seen, great international upheavals bring about either military coups or abrupt, temporary military withdrawals that soon give way to further coups, while periods of stability strengthen military regimes. Paradoxically, it is precisely through this that the genesis of civilianization (however partial and gradual) is possible and even probable. Therefore, even if the United States gains influence in some key Arab military regimes, as seems likely, it is more than doubtful that it can and will do anything significant through diplomatic means or military aid to further civilianization. What remains is the indirect and rather remote influence of contributing to the stability of the environment of the military regimes. This conclusion about the prospects for, and patterns of, transition to civilian rule may seem a pessimistic assessment. It may only indicate our lack of knowledge about the dynamics of civilianization, the decreasing capacity of the superpowers to affect the internal politics of small powers, or perhaps both.

NOTES

1. Amos Perlmutter, "The Arab Military Elite," World Politics 22 (January 1970): 291.

2. For comprehensive surveys on the state of the literature, see ibid.; Gabriel Ben-Dor, "The Politics of Threat: Military Intervention in the Middle East," Journal of Political and Military Sociology 1 (Spring 1973); Eliezer Beeri, *Army Officers in Arab Politics and Society* (New York: Praeger, 1969); and George M. Haddad, *Revolutions and Military Rule in the Middle East,* 3 vols. (New York: Speller, 1965, 1971, 1973). See also the references to the Middle East in the recent comprehensive theoretical survey by A. R. Luckham, "A Comparative Typology of Civil-Military Relations," Government and Opposition 6 (Winter 1971).

3. See Perlmutter, "Arab Military"; Ben-Dor, "Politics of Threat"; Beeri, *Army Officers.*

4. See the discussion of the "return to the barracks" (divided into "abdication" and "re-civilianization") in the classic study by S. E. Finer, *The Man on Horseback: The Role of the Military in Politics* (New York: Praeger, 1962), pp. 190-204.

5. Cf. P. B. Springer, "Disunity and Disorder: Factional Politics in the Argentine Military," in Henry Bienen, ed., *The Military Intervenes* (New York: Russell Sage Foundation, 1968).

6. In the sense put forth in Samuel P. Huntington, *Political Order in Changing Societies* (New Haven: Yale University Press, 1968), elaborated upon in Gabriel Ben-Dor, "Institutionalization and Political Development: A Conceptual and Theoretical Analysis," Comparative Studies in Society and History 17 (July 1975). In Huntington's terms, this paper deals with praetorian societies.

7. Cf. the twofold typology in Finer, *Man on Horseback.*

8. P. J. Vatikiotis, *Conflict in the Middle East* (London: Allen & Unwin, 1971), p. xv.

9. See Malcolm Kerr, *The Arab Cold War,* third ed. (London: Oxford University Press, 1971), whence the term has been taken.

10. Cf. Nadav Safran, "The War and the Future of the Arab-Israeli Conflict," Foreign Affairs 52 (January 1974).

11. Eliezer Beeri, "Changes in the Egyptian Army," Monthly Review (Hebrew), (July 1974): 12.

12. Ibid.

13. Ibid., p. 13.

14. Itamar Rabinovich, *Syria Under the Ba'th 1963-66: The Army-Party Symbiosis* (Jerusalem: Keter, 1972). For a different view, see Amos Perlmutter, "From Obscurity to Rule: The Syrian Army and the Ba'th Party," Western Political Quarterly 12 (December 1969).

15. For an excellent demonstration of how the failure to tackle these problems brought down a military regime, see Uriel Dann, *Iraq under Qassem* (New York: Praeger, 1969).

16. Cf. Richard H. Dekmejian, "The Egyptian Power Elite," paper delivered at the annual meeting of the Middle East Studies Association of North America, Toronto, 1969.

17. The internal turmoil caused by opposite conditions is well brought out for Syria in Patrick Seale, *The Struggle for Syria* (London: Oxford University Press, 1965).

18. Cf. Ergun Ozbudun, *The Role of the Military in Recent Turkish Politics* (Cambridge, Mass.: Harvard University Center of International Studies, 1965); and Walter F. Weiker, *The Turkish Revolution of 1960-1961* (Washington, D.C.: Brookings Institution, 1963).

19. In this sense, the advance of civilianization will mean that the military will make fewer decisions about political personnel and will concentrate instead on fixing the rules with which the personnel must conform.

20. Cf. Dankwart A. Rustow, "The Army and the Founding of the Turkish Republic," World Politics 11 (July 1959).

21. See ch. 1, "Political Change and the Nation State," in Leonard Binder, *The Ideological Revolution in the Middle East* (New York: John Wiley, 1964).

22. The preliminary character of the analysis does not permit a more detailed argument showing a similarity of civilianization in the various Arab countries. However, the common historical background, similar political culture, high interdependence, intensive mutual demonstration effect, and the experience of the political evolution of these countries since independence make this much more than a plausible assertion. This assertion, like all the others about the future evolution of the Egyptian and Syrian regimes, rests on the assumption that the key factors accounting for the present stage of civilianization (inter-Arab tranquility, stability, self-confidence of the military regimes, the virtual elimination of civilian and military opposition) will continue to operate. The importance of this point, needless to say, cannot be overemphasized.

23. See Uri Ranan, "The U.S.S.R. in the Near East," in Jack H. Thompson and Robert O. Reischauer, eds., *Modernization of the Arab World* (Princeton: Van Nostrand, 1966), and his *The U.S.S.R. Arms the Third World* (Cambridge, Mass.: MIT Press, 1969).

24. Cf. the observations on Africa in Henry Bienen, "Foreign Policy, the Military and Development: Military Assistance and Political Change in Africa," in Richard Butwell, ed., *Foreign Policy and the Developing Nation* (Lexington: University of Kentucky Press, 1969).

GABRIEL BEN-DOR is senior lecturer in political science and director of the Institute of Middle Eastern Studies at the University of Haifa.

Transition from Military Rule

The Case of Western State Nigeria

HENRY BIENEN
Princeton University

From the time of military takeover in January 1966, Nigerian military governments on many occasions had asserted their commitment to a return to civilian rule. These assertions were hardly atypical of military regimes in Africa. However, the Nigerian military leaders were frequent in their announcements, spelled out their plans for a return to civilian rule, and took important steps to bring civilians into both state military governments and the federal military government.

From 1967 to 1974, civilians functioned as civil commissioners in the Nigerian federal military government and in state governments. The civilians that were brought into both federal and state levels were a mixed group. Some were individuals who had not been active in politics prior to the 1966 military coups. Others were major politicians either at national or regional levels. For example, Chief Awolowo, a dominant personality in contemporary Nigerian nationalism who was at one time leader of the Western Region and who had also been jailed for treason in 1962, entered the federal government in 1967 as did Aminu Kano, one of the major opponents of the civilian Nigerian Peoples Congress regime in the Northern Region.

What follows is a report on politicians under a military regime.[1] It is a field report on deposed leaders, some of whom reentered politics under military auspices, but who did so very much for their own purposes. It was possible to carry out interviews with these politicians precisely because

---

AUTHOR'S NOTE: *I am grateful for the support of the Rockefeller Foundation, the Woodrow Wilson School, and the Center of International Studies at Princeton University.*

Nigeria is not a police state. Individuals talked freely about their attitudes and roles once guaranteed anonymity, and many people did not even care about being identified.

THE INTERVIEW DATA

From September 1972 to June 1973, we collected data on politicians under a military regime in Nigeria. Our aim was to reveal the realities of military rule in Nigeria from the perspectives of an elite partially cut off from power. We interviewed two sets of politicians. One group consisted of former members of the Western House of Assembly from the old Western Region. We interviewed 54 of the surviving 128 members of the Western House who had served in the turbulent years 1960-1966.

All interviews were carried out by me and my colleague at the University of Ibadan, Martin Fitton. Interviews were typically from 2 to 4 hours long. Sometimes we were both present; at other times only one of us was present during the interview. All interviews were carried out in English. Generally, the Yoruba politicians spoke English with a range of fluency. We had a structured questionnaire, but we often departed from the order of the questions. The interviews were in depth and sometimes an individual was reinterviewed. Interviews were carried out in homes, offices, and places for recreation. Our sample concluded a wide and representative range by party affiliation, age, occupation, and geographical location.

During the period 1960-1966, Nigerian politics was in almost constant crises. The Western Region, with about ten million people, was the scene of intense factional and party struggle.[2] The ruling Action Group (AG), which had dominated nationalist politics in the West and which was led by Chief Awolowo, split in 1962. A rump faction, led by Chief Akintola, who subsequently became premier of the West and was assassinated in the first military coup of January 1966, took over the government of the Western Region after a period of administration by the federal government. Akintola formed a new party, the Nigerian National Democratic party, by bringing new people into politics and by using the carrot and stick to bring into his party former AG politicians and politicians from the National Congress of Nigerian Citizens (NCNC) which more and more became a party of the Ibo-dominated Eastern Region.

Internal struggle among the Yoruba in the Western Region became inextricably tied to regional maneuvering in the Nigerian federation. The Northern-dominated federal government increasingly had to prop up its ally in the West, the Akintola regime. Personal and political animosities became very bitter. The Western election of 1965, like the 1964 federal election in the West, was marked by violence and chicanery. Violence in the West and breakdown of government there were the primary causes of military intervention in 1966.[3] In brief, this is the background to our interviews with members of the Western House of Assembly (MHAs), one source of politicians.

The other source of politicians that we interviewed consisted of those people who served as civilian commissioners in the military governor's cabinet.[4] From 1967 to 1971, the then-Brigadier Robert Adeyinka Adebayo, governor of the Western State which had been created when Nigeria was broken from a federation of four regions into a twelve-state system, ruled with a cabinet made up of civilians. Many of these civilians were former politicians who had served in either the Western House of Assembly, the National Assembly or both.

These commissioners held various portfolios such as lands and housing, finance, local government and chieftaincy affairs, health, and so forth. Heading certain statutory boards at various times gave one commissioner rank and cabinet status. The police chief of the Western State, the general officer in command of the troops in the Western State, and the attorney general were members of the cabinet. We interviewed twelve cabinet members of the twenty who could be considered to have had cabinet status between 1967-1971.

Our aim in carrying out these interviews was to examine the interrelationships between military and civilian personnel. We rejected at the start the idea that dichotomizations of regimes as military or civilian would be very useful. We can define a regime to be a military one if certain conditions are met, but we should bear in mind that "civilian" is a rather large residual category; thus, we should be looking at the various group and institutional alliances that are made across the civilian-military boundary lines. Nigeria provided a good setting for looking at civilian-military relationships because we were able to interview politicians and because the military was relying on civilians to perform important political functions.

Politicians were a group whose support or opposition might be critical to the success of a military regime. If we could find out what they were doing politically, if we could find out how they viewed the regime and their own past, present, and future roles, we could better understand some of the possibilities of transition from military rule or prospects for the maintenance of a military regime. We could better analyze the real-world situation of ongoing civilian-military relations.

Interviews with the MHAs allowed us to get at the attitudes and functioning of grass-roots politicians while the idea in examining cabinet government in the Western State was to look at decision-making under a military regime. Cabinet members were able to make comparisons between the way they operated as politicians in a civilian regime with their activities under a military head of government. This was possible since the cabinet in the Western State was not a cabinet of technicians or professionals. Although it had some doctors and a university professor, it was a highly political body. Most of the commissioners had been prominent politicians during the 1960s, or even much earlier, and were still major figures in Western State political life. If discussions with MHAs would hopefully allow us to say something about middle-level politics under a military regime, interviews with cabinet members would enable us to comment not only on the interaction of high-level civilian politicians and military men, but also on the relationship of civil servants to both military and civilian politicians.[5]

We present some findings below. Because of limitations of space, these findings are cut away from the context of Nigeria as a federal republic. They are to some extent cut away from the recent political history of Western State Nigeria. All that we can say about that history here is that Nigeria's military leadership needed civilians, both civil servants and politicians, in the running of the country. Prior to military rule in 1966 there had been a good deal of social mobilization and political participation. There were parties of long standing prior to 1966. Many regional and national elections had been held in the decade 1956-1966. As mentioned, the country had been in turmoil since 1962. While politicians had been discredited in the eyes of many people by 1966, political networks were still viable. These points have special force for the Western State.

BACKGROUND POLITICAL HISTORY

The problems for military governors in the West were more intense than for those of other parts of Nigeria. The West had gone through a period of extended crises from 1962 to 1965. Elite factionalism was extremely bitter and was expressed in party struggle and by internal splitting within the parties. After the first coup in January 1966, the AG had a leadership, but its paramount leader, Chief Awolowo, was in jail. His strength in what was left of the AG was great enough that he could delegate nominal leadership. Without Awolowo, there would have been much more fragmentation of AG leadership.

In the Nigerian National Democratic party, there was no clear-cut leadership left after the January coup. The former NNDP leader, Akintola, was dead. The deputy leader of the NNDP, Fani-Kayode, had been a leader of the National Congress of Nigerian Citizens prior to joining the NNDP. He himself had challenged Akintola's leadership before the coup and he was not widely accepted by NNDP people. Many NNDP leaders were in hiding or keeping a low profile. The NCNC had been shattered when most of it moved into the NNDP in 1964-1965.

There was certainly no clear-cut civilian leadership, apart from Chief Awolowo himself, that the military government in the West could turn to. Moreover, the splits in the West had by no means been confined to a leadership struggle over spoils of office. The elites of power in Western Nigeria had been able to mobilize nonelites for political struggle. And there is good evidence that conflict in the Western Region was not solely an elite phenomenon. Intra-Yoruba conflict took place over distributions of goods and services which affected large numbers of people. Farmers who wanted roads built in their areas, and people who wanted schools, hospitals, and so forth participated in a struggle for spoils. There were also felt differences over whether one was an Ijebu, Ibadan, Ijesha, Ekiti, Egba, or Ondo Yoruba. These differences permeated the masses. Yoruba were and are internally split by ethnic group distinction and religious differences inside the wider ethnic-language group. Local conflicts over chiefly lineages penetrate deeply too. Elites often encouraged such conflicts, using them to organize support. But this does not mean that the cleavages were somehow phony or that a false consciousness prevailed among the masses because nonclass distinctions were important politically.

Thus, a military government in the West faced a politically mobilized population. It operated in a context where the West was still relatively well-off, vis-à-vis the rest of Nigeria, by income and education, but the comparative advantage was diminishing. The West in 1966 was conscious of the odd-man-out role it had played in independent Nigeria and the pivotal role it could play in the future. Army officers themselves were conscious of past history and future possibilities. In fact, they were especially conscious of the weak Yoruba position in the then-10,000-man Nigerian army at both officer and enlisted men ranks. There were high-level Yoruba officers, but not enough middle-level ones. Thus, the three military governors between 1966 and 1974, Fajuyi,[6] Adebayo, and Rotimi,[7] stressed the need for the West to be unified as it faced the future. Said diplomatically, this meant the West should be a model of unity for the country as a whole. But bluntly said, the West had to be unified as it confronted other areas of Nigeria. And, between 1967-1970, the country had a civil war that was raging.

For the Yoruba military in the West then, there were overriding problems. One was political unity among civilians. The other was the weakness of the Yoruba position in the armed forces nationally and in the West itself, for troops from the North were stationed in the major political and strategic centers of the West. A major demand of Western civilian leaders was for the removal of non-Western troops from the West and an increase in Yoruba in the armed forces. These demands were met between 1967-1969. But the timing of the demands and the way they were to be voiced were not always agreed on by civilian and military leaders. High-level officers felt that the Yorubaization of the army in the West had to be done, but that it was not in the best interests of political leaders to come out and say so since it was the Yoruba officers whose lives were at stake. This was but one example among many of the interaction of civilians and military on critical issues where there was agreement on goals, but not on process.

Many issues were debated privately among the military and civilians. It was necessary, however, to create forums in which issues could be discussed and politics could be explained. It was necessary to have these forums because many individuals had been involved at various levels in Yoruba politics. Support had to be mobilized from below in the face of a national crisis from 1966 to 1970. It also had to be mobilized among district elites and at the center of Yoruba politics. Civilians and military needed each other.

Less than a month after he became military governor of the Western State, in July 1966, Adebayo began to address groups of chiefs and notables to widen his base of support. The Leaders of Thought was created as a consultative body. It provided a forum for Chief Awolowo who had been released from jail by Gowon after the second coup.

More than 80% of the MHA sample at least had been invited to be a Leader of Thought (see Table 1).

Luckham asserts that it was the military leaders and their civil service advisers who made the final decisions for Nigeria at the end of 1966 and through 1967 which led to the civil war.[8] This may be true for the federation as a whole. In the West, however, the Leaders of Thought discussed the critical issues and civilians played a major role both there and in meetings of the Ad Hoc Constitutional Conference which met in Lagos starting in September 1966. The delegates to the conference were selected, according to Luckham, by military governors, and by Leaders of Thought.[9] From the West, Awolowo led the delegation.

During 1967-1969, both civilians and the military vied for power in the West as civil war went on in the country. Indeed, the very day that

TABLE 1
WERE YOU A LEADER OF THOUGHT?

	Number	Percentage[a]
No	6	11
Yes	29	53
Was invited but did not attend	16[b]	30
NA	3	6
	54	

a. All percentages are rounded and do not always sum to 100%.
b. Of the 16 who were invited but did not attend, none were AG, 1 was NCNC, and all the rest were NNDP. Of those who said they were never Leaders of Thought, 2 were AG (as compared to 11 AG identifiers who said they were Leaders of Thought) and the other 4 were NNDP as compared to 15 NNDP people who said they were in Leaders of Thought. Some NNDP people said they used to get invitations one day after the meetings. It was clear that the Leaders of Thought was dominated by the old Action Group leaders.

Western civilian commissioners were sworn in—June 30, 1967—the Biafran leader, Colonal Ojukwu declared that he would wage open war on Nigeria, and one day later, he was dismissed as governor of the East Central State (Nigeria had already been turned into twelve states) and dismissed from the Nigerian army. The civil war which proceeded during summer 1967 threatened the West itself as the neighboring Midwest was occupied by Biafran troops in early August.

Although Awolowo had threatened to lead the West to secession if the East should secede, he did not. On the contrary, Awolowo joined the federal Executive Council in June 1967, as vice-chairman of the council and commissioner for finance in the federal government. But this post gave Awolowo a virtual prime ministership in the federal Executive Council. While he had used the Leaders of Thought to constrain the military in the West, the federal military government and the Western military government had coopted Awolowo too. In the critical months from August 1966 to August 1967, a loose dyarchy of military and civilian government existed in the West. The bargain was struck: the West would support the federal government's demand for a unified Nigeria. Civilians would enter both the federal Executive Council and the state executive councils.

It was clear that the Leaders of Thought was dominated by Awolowo. But it was also true that military officers attended and even addressed meetings; civil servants attended too. It was most active between August 1966, and August 1967—most of the respondents agreed that it fizzled out in 1968. The introduction of the civilian commissioners into the cabinet made the Leaders of Thought unnecessary for the mobilization of both elite and mass support. Moreover, the military governor had a clear interest in diluting the strength of Awolowo and the Action Group. By bringing non-AG people into his cabinet, he broadened his base and ended his reliance on the AG alone. Awolowo was now playing a federal role and his own attention was deflected somewhat from the concentration on the West.

I have noted that on June 30, 1967, then-Brigadier Adebayo, governor of the Western State, appointed civilian commissioners to his cabinet. Brigadier Adebayo's government was defined as a military one because the head of government was in this position by virtue of appointment by the head of the federal military government, General Gowon. The authority came from the head of state and the Supreme Military Council which ruled by decree. But the commissioners who entered Brigadier Adebayo's government, the civil servants who operated at the highest level of the Western State government, and Governor Adebayo himself, did not agree among themselves about the nature of this military government. They did not agree on what the government *ought* to be or what their own roles were in it: that is, they disagreed over whether the cabinet should be executive or merely advisory to the governor. Indeed, they disagreed after the fact whether it had functioned in advisory or executive capacities; over what representation was supposed to mean in a brigadier's cabinet; over the civilian commissioners' relationships to civil servants—again, both over what ought to be and what had been the case between 1967-1971. Nor did they agree on the political functioning of military officers, aside from the governor.

They did agree, however, that Adebayo had politically balanced party, province, and district concerns in his appointments of commissioners. And they agreed that civil servants were salient in the military government. We have already noted that the former members of the Western House of Assembly were extremely conscious of the role of civil servants.

We asked them the questions: Who has gained most from the military regime? Do most civil servants want a return to civilian rule? Do civil servants have different relationships with officers than they had with civilians in the past? The answers were all self-supplied; we made no suggestions regarding individuals or groups.

RESPONSES

The majority of MHAs felt that civil servants had gained in power during the military regime and did not want a return to civilian rule. It was

TABLE 2
POLITICIANS' PERCEPTIONS OF CIVIL SERVANTS IN A MILITARY REGIME

	Number	Percentage (out of 54 respondents)[a]
Who has gained most from the military regime?		
The military	10	19
The civil servants	13	24
The North	6	11
The West	1	2
The people	3	6
NA	21	39
Women contractors	3	6
Minorities	1	2
	58	
Do most civil servants want a return to civilian rule?		
Yes	5	9
No	30	57
They can say	3	6
Don't know	3	6
NA	12	22
They don't	1	2
	54	
Do civil servants have different relationships with officers than they had with civilians in the past?		
No	4	7
Yes[b]	6	11
They have more power	29	54
They had more power at first, not now	3	6
NA	10	19
They have less power	1	2
Can't tell	1	2
	54	

a. More than one answer was sometimes given.
b. Most of the "Yes" responses seemed to indicate that civil servants were more influential under the military regime, but the response was not clear-cut so we made a distinction between "Yes" and "more power."

the cabinet members, however, who interacted with civil servants day-to-day in the ministerial duties and who participated with certain key civil servants in cabinet deliberations. It was they who were involved in sorting out the relationships between political people, civil servants, and the governor.

Some of the cabinet members stressed the importance of their own personal relationships with civil servants rather than any change in basic authority relationships with the coming of a military regime. Other commissioners felt that the civil servants dominated relationships with military officers and civilian commissioners alike.

Personal relations with permanent secretaries were important. At the same time, the commissioners felt they had to master their civil servants. Of course, this is a feeling that ministers in civilian regimes often have too. But the fact that it was a military regime meant that commissioners did not have a direct constituency base, and they felt this even though some believed that political criteria counted for their appointment. They felt a lack of authority because there had been no electoral mandate. They also knew that civil servants had a different attitude in the military regime and would feel freer in going to the governor directly at least some permanent secretaries felt this way.

The high-level civil servants we interviewed sometimes expressed suspicion of the military, yet they recognized the new roles the civil service played in a military regime. They had more leeway and they operated more independently on state boards and corporations. Most insisted that civil servants could serve either under a military government or a civilian one and that it was important for civil servants to have the public and the politicians perceive this. The interviews, however, suggest that MHAs did not have the view that the civil servants were indifferent whether their masters were military or civilian.

Politicians were able to distinguish among military regimes in Nigeria and to differentiate the military's performance in policy realms. Politicians were skeptical about the notion of "the" military. They treated the military as a differentiated group and tended to personalize military politics—as they tend to personalize all politics in Nigeria. They felt that the military had been most successful in bringing about stability by creating a twelve-state system in Nigeria and breaking Nigeria away from the old regional system. They believed the military did not try to be representative, and they gave it rather poor marks in the field of economic and social policy formulation and execution.

About 25% of the MHAs felt that the military had been more successful than civilians in bringing about stability; less than 17% thought the military had been more successful than civilians in bringing about economic development; 15% saw more military success in health and educational areas; and 9% thought the military had been more successful in representing the people than civilians.

TABLE 3
POLITICIANS' PERCEPTIONS OF MILITARY INTENTIONS

	Number	Percentage
Do most officers want a return to civilian rule?		
Yes	4	7
No	26	48
Not sure	3	6
If their interests are gratified	1	2
NA	20	37
	54	
Will there be civilian rule in 1976?[a]		
Yes	8	15
No	23	43
Military cannot be forced to go	5	9
Military does not want to go but it will be forced out	4	7
Don't know	12	22
NA	2	4
	54	
Will military men seek election under a civilian regime?		
Yes	12	22
Yes some but they won't do well	10	19
No	4	7
Few will	10	19
It is their right; they are Nigerians	7	13
NA	11	20
	54	
Should the military have a veto over a civilian regime?		
Yes	4	7
No	28	52
We have a mixed system now	1	2
NA	21	39
	54	

a. This was asked in 1972-1973 as were all questions. Thus the question was asked well before General Gowon announced that the military would not leave in 1976.

In what ways the military would withdraw, if at all, was a major question for politicians. Their estimation of the future role of the Nigerian armed forces in political life was critical to the way they behaved from 1966 on. Whether and in what ways to make one's peace with the military, whether to form alliances with soldiers, whether to wait the military out, whether to surface politically and even overtly to oppose state governments or the federal government—these were questions which faced politicians. Future careers and even lives could be at stake in the way they were answered. Thus, we asked MHAs about the prospects of the military giving way to civilian rule.

The cabinet members we interviewed were less skeptical that the military would go. Four said clearly that the military would be forced to go; "They'll have to leave. Nigeria can't tolerate a dictatorship. More than ten years of rule is impossible." One said that in the West and the North there was a strong agitation to hand over the government to civilians. "They will have no choice unless they want another coup." Another thought that the situation was unpredictable. Someone who had been fairly positive about military rule said: "We can only hope; there is nothing to suggest they won't." This view was repeated by yet another former commissioner. A different ex-commissioner thought that the whole matter was purely speculative, but said that so far there was no statment or even an implied threat that the military would not leave.

On the other side, only one former commissioner firmly said that the military would not go in 1976. "You deceive yourself. Gowon is not keen on going." One said that the common man was indifferent whether there was a military government or not and was satisfied with the performance of the military regime which could not be pushed out in any case. He himself expressed a certain skepticism whether the military would go. A high-level civil servant voiced his skepticism, also.

A greater proportion of the cabinet members was more likely to perceive a good chance of the military's departure than the MHAs. The cabinet members who did think the military would go weighted certain factors more heavily than most of the MHAs. They thought that pressure would be brought to bear on the military from strategic sectors of the population, especially students. They seemed to think that civil servants would be less supportive of the military than the MHAs believed. And, former commissioners thought that internal splits in the military worked as a force on military withdrawal. The commissioners who believed this argued that officers would put the unity of the military as the highest priority and that staying in power threatened corporate unity. But internal division can also work against withdrawal from power. Internal splits inside an armed force can lead a military group to stay in power in order to use the state against another military faction. Or, a faction out of power in the army may try and seize the state to wield it against a dominant military group.

We were interested in knowing whether political figures thought that the military would opt for an Ataturk model, that is, whether soldiers who wanted to become directly involved in partisan politics would leave the armed forces and become civilian politicians. Some military officers thought that military governors, and more generally, soldiers who wanted to opt for politics, would have to surrender their uniforms and to vie with politicians.[10] Some cabinet members stated that officers could run because they had money. The common view expressed by the MHAs was that military men did not have strong local roots. They did not always build a large house back in their home area, as politicians had always done even when they were based in the towns. The military man's ties with a home area had become attenuated through postings and barracks life. (This view was supported by one general interviewed who said, "Why should the military spend money on the people? We have no constituency. Few officers will stand [for election].")

CONCLUSIONS

We have seen that politicians played important roles under a military regime, but that they did so while maintaining hostility to the very idea of a military regime. Yet for the most part they perceived the armed forces' unwillingness or inability to return rule to them. Politicians had complicated, rather than simple, views of military performance and of their own relationships to military personnel and the military regime. They focused on the role of civil servants. Those in the cabinet were less skeptical about military withdrawal from rule because they were more conscious of friction within the armed forces. They clearly perceived limits to effective military rule in Nigeria, but they also recognized the military's ability to continue to rule.

While politicians operated within a military-civilian system, they were against institutionalizing a dyarchy. On October 27, 1972, the former president of Nigeria, Dr. Nnamdi Azikiwe, suggested that a military-civilian government should be established for a period of five years at the expiration of the present military government.[11] He argued that without the wisdom and experience of civilians, the military establishment could not rule democratically and that civil rule depended on the military establishment in any form of government. Thus he proposed a combined civilian and military government. The military governor of the Rivers State, Naval Commander Alfred Diete-Spiff, supported the suggestion for a dyarchy after 1976.[12] Other military leaders did not openly respond however, and the press was almost unanimously against Azikiwe's proposals.

We started interviewing shortly after Azikiwe had introduced his proposals and we included the question on military veto over civilian rule to see how MHAs responded to Azikiwe's notions of a military-civilian dyarchy. Many attacked him personally for trying to ingratiate himself with the military and some saw his proposals as involving a trial period supported by military leaders themselves. Repeatedly, MHAs said that a military government should be a military government and a civilian one should be free of fetters by the military. The cabinet members agreed, although Chief Kolawole Balogun, former federal minister and former commissioner under General Adebayo, argued that the gubernatorial offices of president of the republic and governors of the states should be held by senior army officers.[13]

Since civilians already were operating in a military regime, and since the military regime at that time kept stating that there would be a transfer of power to civilians and many civilians already saw a mixed system operating, what the MHAs were saying was that the military should withdraw completely in a legal way. Indeed, they feared, as did many of those who commented on Azikiwe's proposals, that any discussion of a legally mixed system or a transitional interregnum, would give the military an excuse to stay in power. And as we have seen, the politicians feared that the military would stay in power despite all its claims to the contrary. They wanted military withdrawal from authority and they did not see the Nigerian military as being able to compete in electoral politics.

While there would and could be pressures on the military to leave, in the end the politicians felt that the military could not be forced out, but that military men might feel it would be in their own interest to give up ruling.

However, in the aftermath of controversy over a new census—a controversy reminiscent of the one which raged in the 1960s over an earlier census—General Gowon announced the military government's intention to stay in power beyond 1976 on October 1, 1974. General Gowon said that the nation's military leaders had decided it would be "utterly irresponsible to leave the nation in the lurch by a precipitate withdrawal." He stated that the military had not abandoned the idea of a return to civilian rule, but he maintained the ban on political parties that had been in effect since January 1966.[14]

He also announced that military and police personnel would replace civilians as commissioners in the state and federal governments.

Nigeria thus seemed to be another case of aborted transition back to civilian rule from a military regime which had been at least rhetorically committed to civilian rule. We have tried to argue on the basis of Western

State case study materials that this would be too simple a view of developments in Nigeria from 1966 to 1974. The military needed civilians and politicians, as well as civil servants, to run a large and complex Nigerian state. This need plus the willingness of politicians to work under a military regime they opposed led to tensions in Nigerian politics. These tensions can be understood better by examining the actual functioning of politicians in more detail than we have done.

Here we concentrated more on reporting attitudes than on describing behaviors. Western State Nigeria and the federal republic as a whole remained for the period under discussion a mixed military-civilian system in which both politicians and civil servants played significant roles. These roles will now be elaborated in the context of a military government that no longer states its immediate intention to hand over the rule to civilians. But the need for civilians has not been diminished; military elites have not yet developed their own networks for handling political cleavages and demands throughout Nigeria. If they try to develop such networks, they will operate in a system where civilian elites are still very active and have been legitimated by the military itself. Transition or no transition from military rule, Nigerian civilian-military politics will be a complicated and delicate game. The military could disengage politicians from open politics and dismiss them from formal governmental roles. But this cannot solve their problems. They are cut off from the grass roots again, and they risk mobilizing wider segments of the civilian population into active opposition.

NOTES

1. This paper is part of a larger study of civilian-military relationships in Western State Nigeria. Here we report selectively on our interviews with politicians. Interviews were also carried out with civil servants and military officers. The wider study is forthcoming as *Politics and Politicians in a Military Regime: Western State Nigeria.*

2. It seemed to make sense to concentrate analyses of civilian-military relations in the Western State rather than in Nigeria as a whole. For one thing, we were both based in Ibadan. This location gave us access to politicians in the Western State. In one year it would not have been possible to carry out the same kind of study all over the federation. Western State, with a population of anywhere between nine to twelve million, depending on whose figures one believes, is larger than most African countries. It has a capital city, Ibadan, with close to two million people and is heavily urbanized by African standards. It has one of the most advanced educational systems and best developed administrative services in Africa.

3. For a discussion of the crises in the West see: B. J. Dudley, *Instability and Political Order: Politics and Crises in Nigeria* (Ibadan: University of Ibadan Press, 1973); John P. MacKintosh, *Nigerian Government and Politics* (Evanston: North-

western University Press, 1966); S. K. Panter-Brick, *Nigerian Politics and Military Rule* (London: Athlone Press, 1970), especially Dudley's chapter on the West. For a discussion on the Nigerian coups see: Robin Luckham, *The Nigerian Military*. (Cambridge University Press, 1971); Anthony Kirk-Greene, *Crises and Conflict in Nigeria,* Volume I (London: Oxford University Press, 1971); S. K. Panter-Brick, op. cit.; N. J. Miners, *The Nigerian Army, 1956-1966* (London: Methuen and Co. Ltd., 1971); Ruth First, *Power in Africa* (New York: Pantheon, 1970), esp. pp. 144-168 and pp. 278-362.

4. In the Western State, the military governor appointed twelve commissioners on June 30, 1967. However, some replacements were made between 1967-1971. Moreover, a number of positions not listed as cabinet posts in the original announcement came to be so considered by at least some of the incumbents and their commissioner colleagues. Certain statutory corporations listed as commissioner posts in 1967 subsequently ceased to be so listed.

5. The role of civil servants in a military regime has come under increasing scrutiny, and more and more military regimes are being described as military-civil service regimes. The civil services' commitment to a return to civilian rule has been in doubt in a number of countries. Our forthcoming study deals with these important issues at greater length. For a discussion of civil service-military relationships see: Edward Feit, "Military Coups and Political Development: Some Lessons from Ghana and Nigeria," World Politics 2 (January 1968): 190. Also see Samuel DeCalo, "Military Coups and Military Regimes," Journal of Modern African Studies 2, 1 (March 1973): 105-128. For an interesting study on Latin America see Guillermo O'Donnell, *Bureaucratic Authoritarian Studies in South American Politics* (Berkeley: University of California, 1973).

6. Lieutenant Colonel Fajuyi was the first military governor of the West; he was appointed after the first coup in January 1966. He was killed in Ibadan along with General Ironsi, the first military head of state in Nigeria, in July 1966, during the second coup.

7. General Adebayo was removed as governor of the Western State by General Gowon in 1971. He was replaced by then-Colonel Rotimi, the general officer in charge of the Western State.

8. Luckham, op. cit., p. 311.

9. Ibid., p. 313.

10. These were the words used by Colonel Bajowa in an interview published in the Sunday Times, July 14, 1974, p. 9.

11. Sunday Times, Lagos, October 29, 1972, pp. 5, 7-9, 16; and Daily Times, Lagos, October 28, 1972, p. 1.

12. Sunday Times, Lagos, November 24, 1972, p. 24.

13. Sunday Sketch, Ibadan, November 10, 1972, p. 3.

14. New York Times, October 2, 1974.

HENRY BIENEN is Professor and Chairman in the Department of Politics and Government at Princeton University.

Civilian Participation Under Military Rule in Uganda and Sudan

NELSON KASFIR
Dartmouth College

Political life does not stop when military regimes come into power in developing nations. Military intervention may result in the suspension, if not the elimination of participatory structures, but the makers of coups cannot decree an end to participation despite their frequent proclamations on the subject. There cannot be a political system without some civilian participation on some issues, though the possibilities vary enormously.

When military personnel take power, they immediately create a dilemma for themselves. Their initial action is invariably to suspend civilian political activity in order to prevent the former civilian leaders from rallying support—possibly with the assistance of their civilian political opponents, or friendly factions within the armed forces. But the new military government must search for new policies to establish its own legitimacy. It is often anxious to find some way to determine the level of support it is receiving from the populace. A dilemma is created by the removal of those structures through which the military might test its own acceptance and perhaps consolidate its support.

In the short run military regimes are likely to take actions popular with large numbers of people. In addition, the absence of serious or widespread

---

AUTHOR'S NOTE: *This paper was delivered at the Conference on Civilian Control of the Military: Myth and Reality in Developing Countries, sponsored by the State University of New York at Buffalo and the Inter-University Seminar on Armed Forces and Society, Buffalo, New York, 18 October 1974. I am grateful to Abdo I. Baaklini, James Mittleman, and Claude E. Welch for their suggestions.*

resistance to the coup is usually taken as a sufficient sign of popular acceptance. But in the longer run the military grows increasingly out of touch unless it can design and implement new participatory structures through which it can maintain its support. In addition, since the norm of popular participation has been universally accepted—at least at the level of rhetoric, military leaders tend to concern themselves with structures to reintroduce some degree of civilian political involvement, whether or not they think involvement serves any useful purpose.

There are dangers in taking these steps since the design of new participatory structures is an unfamiliar task for officers—as it is for most other citizens. If the structures succeed, there is the possibility that the military will be unable to control them. If they fail, the manifest absence of support may prove unsettling for the rulers. Consequently, the military are likely to be hesitant and half-hearted about their new experiments in popular politics. They are likely to try a variety of participatory "experiments," discarding them at the first sign of trouble, expanding them where they seem to redound to the advantage of the regime, but seeking always to maintain as tight a degree of control over these structures as possible.

The few comments by scholars on attempts by African military leaders to build mass parties indicate that these efforts have not had much substance.[1] The pattern of participation in the Ghanaian regime under the National Liberation Council is one of the few African cases to have received sustained treatment.[2] Not only did the NLC establish channels to involve people in politics from the presentation of grievances to the writing of a constitution, but Pinkney offers some evidence of how these structures were used. However, the prompt return of the military to power in Ghana only two years after quitting politics reduces the significance of studying the Ghanaian case in order to learn about civilian control.

Since the prospects for either continued or restored civilian control of the military in African countries can be evaluated as doubtful, there is an air of unreality about discussions of strategies to achieve military withdrawal from politics—however ingenious the suggested steps in those strategies may be.[3] The number of African states under military rule has continued to grow. In the few cases where the military has withdrawn from power, it has soon returned to the presidential office. Even Sierra Leone, the most important current exception to this proposition, presents a doubtful case of civilian control of the military.

Instead, it is relevant to examine what kinds of political participation occur in a military regime in order to obtain a fuller appreciation of the interplay of political forces and a more precise understanding of civil-military relations on particular issues at specific times. What, then, are the participatory structures that military rulers create to take the place of those they have banned? What are their reasons for creating them, and what are the characteristics of the participation these new structures engender? There are various important ways in which civilians are involved in governments run by soldiers. Military rulers, for example, necessarily work with civilian administrators for reasons of both expertise and manpower.[4] There may be much bargaining behind the scenes with important interest groups. And, much of the civilian participation that occurs under military rule is shadowy and outside established procedures precisely because military leaders believe they are not engaging in politics.

The new participatory structures, on the other hand, are necessarily public, as are the responses to them. Consequently, they are easier to examine than the full pattern of participation.

Uganda under President Idi Amin and Sudan under President Ja'afar Nimeiri provide sharply contrasting experiences with the problems of establishing new modes of civilian participation under military rule. Both regimes have changed their approach sharply. Both leaders have had good reason to feel insecure during the entire period they have been in office. The Ugandan military government has introduced and then discarded a variety of participatory structures with bewildering speed, and as a result has progressively reduced civilian participation. The second Sudan military government, on the other hand, began with relatively low levels of civilian involvement, but has since expanded them to an extraordinary degree. Under what circumstances, then, will civilian political participation be sufficiently attractive to the officers who rule that they will introduce a substantial measure of participation in what is nominally a military regime?

UGANDA: CONSTRICTING CIVILIAN PARTICIPATION

The value the military regime of Idi Amin placed on civilian political participation was never greater than in the first months after the coup in January 1971. Amin's immediate problem upon taking power grew out of the fact that his coup was as much against an important segment of the army as it was against the civilian regime of Milton Obote. Efforts to ease Amin out of the chain of command and to isolate him from his supporters within the army had become public six months before, though they had begun considerably earlier.[5] In that situation the armed forces could be regarded as two rival factions, one centering around Obote, the other around Amin, though there is evidence to suggest that these factions were most likely unstable coalitions of even smaller groups (to some extent reflecting the complex cleavages in the Ugandan political and social system).

Factionalism in the Ugandan army appears to have been the product of several considerations dating back to independence. In 1962 Uganda had approximately 1,000 soldiers under arms. Due to external security problems with Sudan, Zaire, and Rwanda, as well as internal security problems with Karamojong and Turkana cattle raiders, and disorder in Sebei, Buganda, Bunyoro, and the Ruwenzori mountains, the number of soldiers grew at a rate of more than 40% a year for the next five years—faster than anywhere else on the continent.[6] The speed of growth seems likely to have reduced disciplined obedience to the line of command and thus to have facilitated factional coalitions.

Equally significant in the long run was the promotion of non-commissioned officers to higher ranks. This tendency can be dated back to the 1964 mutiny at the Jinja barracks, but has grown steadily to the present when former NCOs hold virtually all key commands and a majority of the lower positions. The mutiny, said to have been led by an NCO, occurred shortly after the number of direct-entry officers grew larger than the number of NCOs.[7] The direct-entry officers possessed higher levels of formal education, but far less experience than the NCOs. Opportunities for rapid promotion would occur when the British officers who held almost all commissioned positions were replaced. The longer the NCOs waited, the less claim they could make for those positions.

The mutineers demanded higher pay and rapid Africanization of the officer corps. They held the defense minister, Felix Onama, hostage to underline these demands. As in Tanzania, however, they made no overt move against the civilian government. Amin, who had been promoted through the ranks, was flown home from a course in England to take command of the First Battalion in an effort to quell the mutiny. The Obote government not only met the demands of the mutineers, but even reinstated those who were dismissed for fomenting the mutiny. The political power of the soldiers was amply demonstrated, inviting further indiscipline in later years.

Lee calls attention to the "constant competition between N.C.O.s and the officers" during the 1960s.[8] Indiscipline due to the inability of officers to control their men was widely reported when the army was called out in December 1969 following an attempt on Obote's life. Only 7 of the 14 officers placed in commanding positions by Obote in September

1970 were trained overseas.[9] Under Amin distrust of officers trained abroad has become even more striking.

Amin built his ties in the army through the NCOs. The announcement of the coup on Radio Uganda was made by a Warrant Officer Class II and several sergeants were promoted shortly thereafter. The operational maneuvers for the coup had been planned by Amin and a small group of trusted soldiers for at least a week and were in no sense a spontaneous response to "Acholi and Longi soldiers" arming themselves to take control, as Amin originally claimed.[10] Through his control of the Malire Mechanized Regiment, Amin was able to dominate the brief fighting that occurred in Kampala on the first day of the coup.

Thus, his immediate security task was to destroy the "unreliable elements" in the armed forces. Contrary to the public image of tranquility without victimization for several months followed by massacres in the barracks in Mbarara, Jinja, and Moroto and on a smaller scale elsewhere in July 1971, two officers (Brigadier Hussein and Lieutenant Colonel Oyok) were killed, after being taken prisoners, two days after the coup. Many police and army officers, particularly those of Acholi and Langi origin, and hundreds of enlisted men were killed over the new two months. The July massacres accounted for the deaths of at least 1,000 more.[11]

An unguarded comment suggests the dangers of the present level of factional conflict in the Ugandan army. In his affidavit to the Commission of Inquiry inquiring into the deaths of Micholas Stroh and Robert Siedle in the Mbarara barracks, Lieutenant Silver Tibihika remarked that after disposing of the dead Americans' car by pushing it over a cliff 150 miles away from the barracks, his party (consisting of two other officers and twenty recruits) faced a dilemma. "It was then daylight and I was afraid the troops of the unit stationed there might regard us as enemies. . . ."[12] He reported to the commanding officer of the Fort Portal barracks, but his concern suggests the dangers to soldiers in wandering out of their own bailiwick. Amin, in any event, could not rely on a united and obedient army, when he set about the tasks of running a national government, and his position may have grown weaker since.

Following conventional military form, Amin issued decrees dissolving the parliament and district, municipal, and town councils immediately after the takeover.[13] Elections were postponed up to five years, and political parties were banned. With the exception of the new cabinet which consisted primarily of civilians, and the judiciary which was heavily controlled, the pre-coup channels of participation were eliminated.

The coup was greeted with a burst of spontaneous participation in Kampala and nearby districts, as people identified the change of regime with the removal of anti-Baganda measures. Responses upcountry were more subdued.[14] One interesting response that appeared again and again was the use of the letters column in the local newspapers to announce support of a particular group for the military government and then to follow it by requesting the new rulers to rectify a grievance felt by members of that group. At one point the President's Office asked in a local newspaper that members of the public direct their requests to particular ministries, as the President's Office could not cope with so many. In part this level of unchanneled participation reflects the degree to which the Obote government had closed down the possibilities of effective participation by its last year.

The Amin government took several steps to gain legitimacy in its first months. The "eighteen points" given as justification for the coup skillfully included most grievances on the minds of Ugandans at the time. The government publicly invited the support of officials close to Obote and appointed many of them to high positions. The new regime agreed to bring the body of the former Kabaka back to Uganda for burial. Of the 92 detainees then held by the government, 55 were released in a public ceremony. The state of emergency was lifted. Amin went out of his way to consult the former kings and constitutional heads. He even released one from prison. Two districts were created by dividing Acholi and Karamoja in half—the first new ones since independence. The government also introduced heavier penalties for *kondos* (armed robbers)—a popular move.

During its early stages officials of the military government felt that it was highly desirable to make contact with the people as visibly as possible—partly to emphasize the failure of the UPC government to maintain effective participation. Amin traveled all over the country, as did his ministers, to explain at length that his was a government of "action, not words." He also offered to "settle" many of the intractable disputes that previously seemed to have made it far more difficult to promote grievances publicly. Promising a solution seemed a good way to gain support in the short run from both sides to still smouldering disputes.

The government staged and publicized a series of conferences generally attended by Amin in which members of conflicting groups were encouraged to put their grievances on the table and to bargain them out. Amin's efforts to "settle" the Rwenzururu dispute between the minority Bakonzo and Baamba, who wanted either a separate district or secession from Uganda, and the Batoro was typical. During the previous regime the

Baamba and Bakonzo had protested the government's refusal to meet their demands with every conceivable tool from petitions to violent armed attacks. These protests had not budged the government and many Bakonzo and Baamba had given up the struggle. Amin offered to mediate this "100 year old dispute" by gathering together the original and to some extent discredited leaders from both sides and offering them an official (though temporary) forum.[15] Feelings on both sides quickened. When he failed, he publicly turned the dispute over to a commission of inquiry that never met.

A similar technique of a series of conferences politicized existing religious cleavages. These have contributed heavily to political conflict in Uganda since the wars of the religious parties in Buganda in the late 1800s. Obote had previously used the resources of his government to set up rival religious bodies in order to build support for the Uganda Peoples Congress, but he also used government sanctions to prevent these issues from becoming the basis of participation after 1966. Shortly after the coup Amin convened a conference at Kabale and another at Kampala for leaders of all major religious groups. He also set up a department of religious affairs. Conflicts in the Protestant and Muslim establishments were publicly aired in further meetings.

Half a year after taking power the government took another initiative to set up a channel for civilian participation. In place of the district councils that had been dissolved, councils of "elders" were established. The format was strongly reminiscent of colonial notions of reinforcing indirect rule by strengthening traditional councils or creating new ones bearing traditional trappings.[16] As with most other ventures of the Amin regime, there was considerable confusion over the functions, membership, and formal position of these councils. The number of elders seemed to vary from one occasion to another. It was not even clear whether they represented administrative districts or ethnic units.

At first, the district commissioners were told to select local notables for the councils. Later, in the last important meeting of an elders' council, Amin conceded, following discussion with some rather vocal elders:[17]

> that it is the people themselves who should determine as to who their representatives ought to be. But the district commissioners, the saza chiefs, the gombolola chiefs, the muluka chiefs and the batongole must sit with you on councils for the selection of representatives. These representatives will be in direct contact with the government. It is through them that government will reach the people.

Nothing ever seems to have been done about this, however.

As one might expect, the military government tended to use the councils of elders to legitimize their own decisions as much as it permitted them to forward demands of the people of an area. The councils seemed to be a two-way channel with Amin deciding which issue would be treated in one way or the other. On occasion the government thanked elders for the memoranda they had "previously" submitted, after a national policy had been announced. In one instance "General Amin again thanked the Elders of Koboko for their advice as how to handle the Church leaders from Namirembe and West Buganda Dioceses."[18] In another case an attempt to overthrow the state was "revealed" to the government in a "memorandum" submitted by "Alur and Jonam elders."[19]

However, the Baamba and Bakonzo elders, the Kigezi elders, and the Baganda elders among others have taken advantage of their opportunity and made some demands on the government through this forum. After their abortive conference with Amin, the Baamba and Bakonzo elders continued to submit memoranda laying out the case for a separate district, and requesting that their languages be used on Radio Uganda. Broadcasts in Lukonzo were introduced for a time. The Kigezi elders apparently requested a variety of projects including a new police post and aid to private schools. Amin responded by announcing that the government had provided solutions to some of these problems.[20]

In August 1971 the high point of the councils of elders was reached when Amin invited the Baganda elders to a meeting to discuss their grievances. Twelve hundred of them showed up and promptly demanded the restoration of the Kabakaship.[21] While Amin had announced that there would be no return to kingdoms as early as the day after the coup, he now indicated that he would appoint a committee to look into the possibility. He also pointed out that kings were costly and might reintroduce divisive political issues. He then asked the elders in other districts to offer their opinions. The issue of the restoration of kingship may have been a decisive one in terms of whether Amin was going to rely significantly on civilian support. That would have meant ruling with the Baganda and hoping to retain his hold on the army, despite the negative reaction of many soldiers.

Two weeks later statements were sent by several councils stating that they did not want their own constitutional heads (the equivalent of a king) back and were against the reestablishment of the Kabakaship.[22] Their reasons were identical to those Amin had given two weeks earlier. Whether Amin had arranged for the councils to send messages to back up his own position, or whether these were an expression of anti-Baganda feeling—one of the few points on which most areas outside Buganda can unite—remains unclear. In any case Amin warned the Baganda elders not to raise the issue of restoration again.[23]

Few issues in Uganda are more potent than kingship. It is an issue on which people in all areas, whether they once were ruled by kings or not, feel strongly. Members of the armed forces who gained a measure of prestige by defeating one king in 1966 are also thought to reject the return of kings out of hand. The dangerous potentialities in publicized elders councils resulting from this issue cannot have been lost on Amin.

The device of councils of elders was extended to other groups to whom Amin wished to announce or discuss a particular policy. In December 1971 Asian "elders" were summoned to a conference, and just prior to the departure of the Israelis in March 1972, Amin called their "elders" in for a meeting. The device seems to have slowly fallen in disuse since.

With the expulsion of the Asians and the invasion of the guerrilla force supporting Obote (September 1972) the military government has reduced the low-level intermittent civilian participation it encouraged earlier. The expulsion was a popular move at first, though the effect dissipated as Ugandans became disgruntled when the pattern of allocation of the abandoned Asian businesses and properties became apparent. Members of the army seem to have gained greatly from this shift of resources. Originally, boards of civilians, primarily ministers, were assigned the task of determining who would receive each business. But they were abruptly replaced by army officers before the allocation process was completed.

The largely civilian cabinet has been replaced by one dominated by military officers. For some time, however, it seems that the defense council, made up entirely of military men, has made most important policy decisions. In a remarkable exercise in March 1973 almost all of the chiefs in the country were dismissed and replaced in "elections." When many of the old chiefs were reelected, Amin canceled many of the results and ordered new elections run this time by military officers. Little has appeared to indicate that these "elections" were not managed. In some areas military men became the chiefs. In early 1974 district administration was completely reorganized dividing the 18 that existed when the coup took place to 38 districts grouped within 10 provinces. Of the first 10 provincial governors, 8 came from the military, one from the police, and one from the prisons service.

A number of possible explanations might be offered for the inability or unwillingness of the military government to sustain structures through which a modest level of civilian participation might be maintained continuously, instead of the haphazard unpredictable encouragement it has received. Perhaps the most plausible is that the armed forces have never overcome the factionalism that marked their development since independence. Amin's concern to outwit those plotting coups against him permits few opportunities to promote civilian participation. Furthermore, the constant insecurity among the military accentuates the dangers posed for civilians who enter the public eye by engaging in participatory activity. Of equal importance perhaps is the lack of personal interest Amin now takes in promoting civilian participation.

SUDAN: ENCOURAGING CIVILIAN PARTICIPATION

The Sudan has experienced an extraordinary flowering of structures designed to elicit civilian political involvement over the past five years. Sudan, by contrast with Uganda, is undergoing its second experience with military rule. To a certain extent the military rulers are reacting to the failures of the regime of General Ibrahim Abboud that culminated in its overthrow in October 1964 by popular demonstrations backed by a radical group of junior officers. To some degree they are also reacting to the failure of the radicals and professionals who guided the October "revolutionary" government but then lost control of it to the more traditionally inclined old-line political parties. Most important, however, has been the change in the composition of the top policy makers in Nimeiri's government from those favoring limited mobilization on the basis of ideological commitment to those preferring mass involvement through relatively open access. As of 1974, however, it is not clear that the present regime is any more secure than is Amin's government in Uganda.

The first coup in Sudan occurred two years after independence following the intricate maneuvering of the leaders of the National Unionist, Peoples Democratic, and Umma parties, all of whom gave the public impression of being more interested in gaining power than in maintaining their political principles. Whether the Abboud coup was the result of the military taking power or having it thrust upon them by Abdullah Khalil, then the prime minister, is still a disputed point. As in Uganda, this was a "general's" coup. Unlike Uganda, though, the coup was bloodless. It has been called a "coup by courtesy," arranged by Khalil in the hope that he could retain power despite the loss of parliamentary support.[24] In consequence there was an element of civilian participation in the coup itself.

The major initiative of the Abboud government in channeling civilian participation was to organize elections to local government councils. There were 74 of these (18 urban and 56 rural).[25] One-half to two-thirds of the members were elected, and the others were nominated. Above the local councils were provincial councils, drawing some of their members from the local councils, and over these was a central council containing both provincial councilors and government ministers. The system was a form of "guided democracy" similar to that adopted by Ayub Khan in Pakistan. "Control," Ruth First observes, "was exercised from the top.... At no level did elected members command a majority...."[26] On the other hand, important new functions were taken from the district commissioner and given to the local councils.[27]

Upon taking power the Abboud regime banned parties and demonstrations and restricted newspapers that were not under government control. But a series of challenges to the right of the military to rule were mounted. The new government faced several threats from army units during its first two years—partly as the product of civilian political cleavages spilling into the military.[28] These resulted in changes among the military personnel in the Supreme Council, and a loss of confidence among the populace. From 1960 until it fell from power, the Abboud regime also faced a series of popular protests.[29] The residents of Wadi Halfa opposed the government plan to relocate them in Kashim el Girba when their lands were flooded following the completion of the Aswan dam. Shortly afterward, several of the old politicians wrote public letters to Abboud asking when the military would withdraw as they had promised. Twenty-seven thousand railway workers went on strike, as did the Gezira tenants. University of Khartoum students demonstrated against the regime on the anniversary of the army takeover several years running. While none of these events destroyed the ability of the military to govern, they amounted to a significant degree of civilian participation in opposition to the Abboud regime—far in excess of anything that has occurred in Uganda since 1971.

The revolution of October 1964, on the other hand, demonstrated that extensive and sustained civilian participation can bring down a military government. Without cleavages in the army this would not have been possible. But without public demonstrations organized in opposition to army rule it would not have happened either. The revolution was not planned. It began with the refusal of students to disperse when the police attempted to breakup a meeting called to discuss the government's failure to solve the southern problem.[30] Rifle shots were fired and a student was killed. A funeral procession attracted popular support: a United National

Front containing representatives of the old political parties and professionals was formed. The critical events were a general strike in Khartoum and demonstrations in the other towns. General Abboud apparently was shocked to discover just how unpopular the military government had become. There was an attempt to arrange a compromise with Abboud or another top military figure becoming head of an essentially civilian government to avoid blotting the prestige of the armed forces, but radical junior officers refused to support this move.[31] Thus, a civilian government containing representatives of the old parties, but dominated by radically minded professionals, was established.

Domination of the government by radicals lasted three months. The old-line parties, particularly the Umma which brought large numbers of its supporters to Khartoum,[32] forced the cabinet to resign in February. The new cabinet was dominated by conservatives, though Sirr al Khatim al-Khalifa was retained as prime minister. The stage was now set for another round of intraparliamentary competition, perceived by many participants as demoralizing as that which provoked the Abboud coup. While not often agreeing with each other, both radicals and professionals realized that the goals they had supported in the October revolution had been entirely undercut. When their next opportunity arose they took more drastic steps to prevent a conservative reaction.

That opportunity came with the second bloodless coup in May 1969 when Nimeiri and the Free Officer movement took control in the face of a stalemate between the parties. Once again the political parties were formally dissolved and no one was allowed to join the government as a member of another party (which caused particular problems for the Communists who had already swung behind the new military government). From the start, however, unlike the Abboud government and unlike military rule in Uganda, there were demands from inside the government for a new political movement that would be open to civilians.

Two basic decisions to implement this policy were necessary. A set of structures had to be designed and a decision had to be made whether these structures should be opened to popular entry or limited to the ideologically committed.[33] In essence the institutions were designed by leftists—both Communists and Nasser-inspired Arab Socialists—with the intention that these structures be run by militants. But, between late 1970 and late 1972 (while the structures were being organized), a power struggle occurred in which the leftists were eclipsed by more moderate technocratically inclined professionals. This latter group, which contained a higher proportion of civilians, accepted the structures as they were, but opened them up to the populace at large. The issue which Niblock poses, then, is whether the possibility of large-scale civilian participation, which (if it occurs) will necessarily include a predominance of the conservative supporters of the old parties, will force the military to eliminate the new participatory structures or to give up power once again.

In the political struggle to shape national policy, the leftists held the dominant position for the first year and a half, though they quarreled among themselves. The Communists split on the issue of whether to disband and join the Sudan Socialist Union (SSU). They began to lose their positions in November 1970. The coup they staged in July 1971 was an attempt to regain a position they had already lost, not to consolidate their control. Following his restoration in the countercoup three days later, Nimeiri was forced to purge even those Communists who had left the Sudan Communist party and joined the SSU and who were not implicated in the coup. The Arab Socialists held on until January 1972, but were fundamentally out of step with Nimeiri by then and had no support base in the country at large to protect them from dismissal. Nimeiri appears to have been impressed with the popular support he received in the countercoup and thus arranged for a plebescite, perhaps to acquire a popular base. For pragmatic reasons, then, he was prepared to countenance a shift from reliance on the ideologically committed to wider popular support. He may also have been dismayed with the serious economic consequences of the decisions to nationalize businesses and to expand social services taken by his ministers in the first year after the coup.

To replace the leftists Nimeiri called on a number of academics and (Sudanese) civil servants working for international organizations. By and large these were moderate professionals who had no connection with the old political parties. A few more southerners were added after the Addis Ababa agreement. They tended to work closely with the moderate professionals. However, with the exception of the southerners, the professionals do not have an obvious support base in the country.

Nimeiri's popular support may also be narrower than it appears to be at first sight. In March 1970 army units clashed with members of al Ansar on Aba Island, routed them, and forced their spiritual leader, the grandson of the Mahdi to flee to Ethiopia. (He appears to have been killed attempting to force his way across the international border, but no definitive information has been released.) Members of al Ansar have been regarded as opponents of Nimeiri from the time of the coup. The battle may have reduced their ability to overthrow him, but it certainly has also reduced their willingness to give him popular support. On the other side of the political spectrum, the countercoup and subsequent dissolution of all organizations that were Communist-dominated, plus the shift away from the Arab Socialists, have reduced Nimeiri's support base from the left. That leaves him with the army and educated moderates—a tiny, but powerful, segment of Sudanese society.

The first step the government took to develop new participatory structures was to write a "National Charter." It was originally completed in November 1969, revised by a committee, and then ratified by the founding congress of the SSU in January 1972. As the "basic philosophy of the Revolution," it sets forth the essential position of the militants, and consequently now appears to be largely a dead letter.

Popular and functional organizations (unions of workers, farmers, teachers, women, youth, village development committees, and the like) were encouraged where they existed, or were created to permit every sector of the population to express its interests. Many of these organizations held their founding congresses by 1973. In addition local government has been overhauled with councils established by an act decreed in November 1971. Councils are supposed to be set up in every village, town section, market area, and nomadic encampment. All members must be elected, though at least one quarter must be women and other places may be reserved for candidates representing popular and functional organizations. Above this level there are town and rural councils, subprovince and province councils. Members of higher level councils are drawn from representatives from the level below. The intention is to increase mass participation, and as Niblock points out, the number of councils formed thus far is staggering.[34]

The Sudan Socialist Union, the only legal party, was created after the opposition of the Communist party was overcome. A "preparatory committee" set up basic rules and a founding congress was held in January 1972. The structure consists of basic units with a party committee and conference at branch, district, subprovince, province, and national levels. Provincial congresses held meetings in December 1973 and the first National Congress was held in January 1974. Again, the number of subunits organized is extraordinary.[35]

A permanent constitution was adopted in April 1973 following debate by the first People's Assembly. It defines the presidency and the People's Assembly. Both have legislative authority, though the president is intended to be the dominant figure. Both the president and members of the assembly are to be elected. Nimeiri was originally elected to office in a national plebescite held in September and October 1971, following the countercoup that put him back in power.[36]

Two national elections and one regional election—each involving contests in most constituencies—have also been held between 1972 and 1974. The first national election, which took place in November 1972, produced the members of the first People's Assembly (that drafted the constitution). The second one was held in April and May 1974. In the latter case the SSU was required to certify that it did not oppose each candidate before he or she could stand. However, the candidates did not have to belong to the SSU.

The regional election was held in the South in accordance with the Addis Ababa agreement that ended the civil war. One provision of that agreement required that democratic elections be held to fill the People's Regional Assembly (which was created by the agreement). These elections occurred in November and December 1973. Approximately 935,000 people were registered (in a widely dispersed total population of roughly 4 million) to vote in 57 of 60 constituencies—the remaining 3 were filled by appointment of 1 member from the police, prisons, and Army.[37] A total of 349 candidates— ranging from 2 to 28 in each constituency—contested the elections. Winners received from 301 to 17,175 votes, depending on the type of constituency. Only half the seats contested were organized in territorial constituencies; the remainder were contests in constituencies limited to popular and functional organizations or administrative units. In one constituency in which a regional minister seemed to emerge victorious, the existence of fraud was sufficiently demonstrated that the results were canceled and a by-election held. The minister lost the second time around, despite support from Abel Alier (a civilian), the president of the high executive council of the southern region and vice-president of the Sudan.

It is too early to say whether these participatory structures will amount to much meaningful participation. For the moment everyone is so busy organizing everyone else that they have little time for substantive policy discussions below the national and (southern) regional levels. (Perhaps they also have no time available to think about overthrowing the present government.) It seems unlikely that the military government will release the reins when important issues are raised. Rather, the system may become an elaborate form of controled participation in which the military sets the limits of debate.

As of 1974, Nimeiri has far too little political support to think about cutting his own ties to the army. By encouraging wide-ranging participation, he might be able to shift the premises on which large numbers of people are prepared to act so that he can gain support from those currently dissident. But the present (1974) bitterness over rising prices is likely to erode any such advantage. The persistent secondary and university student demonstrations in the latter half of 1973 suggest that more than a few are impatient to return to the glorious days of October 1964.

CONCLUSION

In both Uganda and Sudan military governments committed themselves to civilian participation shortly after taking power. Both introduced structures to facilitate involvement. Both changed the nature of their commitment in mid-course. The Ugandan government abandoned the attempt to create a structure which it never formalized, perhaps in part because the demand presented by the Baganda elders was a threat to the fragile internal balance of power Amin had achieved at that moment. The Sudan government, in contrast, responded to internal political upheavals by expanding the channels for political participation by civilians.

One simple, though sometimes overlooked, explanation is that the leadership in the Sudan is simply more committed at a personal level to civilian involvement than are the rulers in Uganda. The army men holding political power in the Sudan have already experienced the rise and fall of a military government that made little effort to encourage political activity by civilians. Furthermore, they saw the conservative political forces seize control from the progressives and the professionals in 1965, three months after the October revolution. Disillusioned with a strongly ideological expression of progress, the Sudan's military leaders apparently hope to establish a political framework which will educate people away from conservative loyalties rooted in the old religious movements—al Ansar and Khatmiyya. There is also the pragmatic judgment that increasing civilian political participation, particularly in the southern region, gives the military leadership some sorely needed popular support. Southern politicians fear that any overthrow of Nimeiri could lead to a return to civil war.

Ugandan military rulers, on the other hand, have to cope with bitter and overt factionalism in the armed forces on a day-to-day basis. These leaders have little formal education and much distrust for highly trained civilian advisers. They are not prepared, it seems, to accept civilian participation expressed through formally established procedures.

A second element of explanation rests on relating military behavior to the acceptance of basic social norms—in this case the commitment to participation. The military are more likely to hold this value the more strongly it is supported by the civilian educated elite. A comparison of the amount of political participation in Uganda and Sudan when those countries were under civilian control suggests that there was more political activity of all types in the Sudan, as well as more tolerance of that activity. The postindependence history of political participation in Uganda was one of steady decline as more and more people were forced out of politics.[38] Furthermore, the amount of overt political opposition in the form of strikes, demonstrations, public letters, and underground circulars common to both military governments in the Sudan has surprisingly little counterpart in Uganda. The Sudan may be a praetorian society in the sense that many (particularly urban) spheres of life are politicized, while Uganda is not. Thus, the difference in emphasis on civilian participation by the military in the two countries may in part follow from the difference in the degree of acceptance of participation as a societal value.

Whatever explanations are seen as relevant, it is clear that many military governments feel it necessary to introduce structures through which civilians can participate. The forms and levels of participation will vary widely, however, from one military regime to another. The result may be that there emerge political issues on which civilians are likely to possess significant influence and perhaps even control. While military leaders may acquiesce in civilian control of certain policies, there is little evidence from the case of the Sudan and Uganda to suggest that bringing civilians back into the political arena is likely to result in a military exit from power.

NOTES

1. Samuel Decalo, "Military Coups and Military Regimes in Africa," Journal of Modern African Studies 2, 1 (March 1973): 117.

2. Robert Pinkney, *Ghana under Military Rule 1966-69* (London: Methuen and Co., Ltd., 1972).

3. See, for example, Claude E. Welch, "The Dilemmas of Military Withdrawal from Politics: Some Considerations from Tropical Africa," African Studies Review 17, 1 (April 1974).

4. See Robert Dowse, "The Military and Political Development," in Colin Leys, *Politics and Change in Developing Countries: Studies in the Theory and Practice of Development* (Cambridge: Cambridge University Press, 1969), pp. 229-232.

5. In July and August 1970 Amin began to give speeches to the Muslim faction led by Prince Badru Kakungulu, a close relative of the former Kabaka. The UPC government was attempting to build up a rival Muslim group. In September 1970 Amin was rumored to have been put under house arrest, though he attended a Makerere University ceremony in a move that was then taken to be an act of defiance of the government. In September 1970 an Obote supporter in the army, Brigadier Suleiman Hussein, was made army chief of staff (having previously been commander of the First Infantry Battalion), in an attempt to remove Amin from operational command by promoting him to "chief of defense staff." A year before the coup the most important officer supporting Obote, Brigadier Pierino Okoya, was murdered. Amin was widely assumed to have been implicated, though an inquest conducted by Justice Arthur Dickson after Amin became head of state found conflicting evidence, and concluded that Okoya and his wife were killed by "persons unknown." Uganda Argus, June 17, 1971, pp. 1 and 8.

6. J. M. Lee, *African Armies and Civil Order* (London: Chatto & Windus, 1969), p. 105.

7. Ibid., p. 108.

8. Ibid., p. 105.

9. F. J. Ravenhill, "Military Rule in Uganda: The Politics of Survival," African Studies Review 17, 1 (April 1974): 240.

10. The operational maneuvers are discussed in a memorandum prepared for Obote by C. L. Ntende, then permanent secretary to the ministry of internal affairs, later published in The Standard, Tanzania, February 16, 1971. While caution must be exercised in relying on documents issued by those thrown out of office by the military, this one appears to be authentic. In any event Wanume Kibedi, Amin's brother-in-law, and for two years his minister of foreign affairs, says flatly that "the coup was a deliberate and preconceived venture...." "Kibedi Speaks Out," Africa Report 20, 4 (July-August 1974): 45.

Amin's version of the events of the coup was reported in The People, January 27, 1971, p. 1. No solid evidence has been presented to support the numerous claims that Obote relied heavily on certain military and police officers and large numbers of privates on the basis of their ethnic origin.

11. Michael Posner, *Violations of Human Rights and the Rule of Law in Uganda* (Geneva: International Commission of Jurists, 1974), pp. 27-33; The Observer, July 25, 1971, p. 5. After making several denials, Amin deplored the fighting in the barracks in a speech given to a police unit. Uganda Argus, August 17, 1971, p. 1.

12. *Commission of Inquiry into the Missing Americans Messrs. Stroh and Siedle held at the Conference Room, Parliament House, Kampala* (Entebbe: Government Printer, 1972), p. 104.

13. Decrees, Nos 1 and 2 of 1971 (Entebbe: Government Printer, February 2, 1971).

14. Baganda, as an ethnic group, had little or nothing to do with implementation of the coup. A.G.G. Gingyera-Pinycwa, "A.M. Obote, the Baganda, and the Uganda Army," Mawazo (Kampala) 3, 2 (December 1971): 44.

The night after the coup an official announced on Uganda television (in what remains one of my favorite examples of official communications): "The public is informed that the takeover of the Government has been received with great jubilation in Kampala and upcountry." The People, January 27, 1971, p. 8.

[84] POLITICAL PARTICIPATION UNDER MILITARY REGIMES

15. The People, May 4-6, 1971.

16. Use of the councils of elders as participatory structures of a limited sort is one instance supporting Edward Feit's prediction that "the system that will prevail [in future African governments] will, most likely, be an adaptation of administrative and traditional rule along the lines of former colonial government...." "Military Coups and Political Development: Some Lessons from Ghana and Nigeria," in Marion E. Doro and Newell M. Stultz, *Governing in Black Africa: Perspectives on New States* (Englewood Cliffs: Prentice-Hall, 1970), p. 232.

17. Comments following main speech to Buganda elders, in *Speeches By His Excellency The President, General Idi Amin Dada* (Entebbe: Government Printer, 1972), p. 33. Newspaper reports of this speech vary from the translation from Luganda printed here.

18. Uganda Argus, December 14, 1971, p. 5. Koboko is in the old West Nile District, and it seems unlikely that the Alur elders there were closely acquainted with the religious conflicts within the Protestant establishment in Buganda with which Amin was then preoccupied.

19. Uganda Argus, October 14, 1971, p. 1.

20. Uganda Argus, August 21, 1972, p. 8.

21. The People, August 6-7, 1971, p. 1.

22. See Uganda Argus, August 23, 1971, p. 1 (Lango elders), August 25, 1971, p. 1 (Ankole elders, including the former king), and August 27, 1971, p. 5 (Madi elders).

23. Uganda Argus, October 1, 1971, p. 7. See also Amin's "Message to the Nation," delivered at the independence celebrations, October 9, 1971, and reprinted in *Speeches by His Excellency*, pp. 36-39.

24. Ruth First, *Power in Africa* (Harmondsworth: Penguin, 1971), pp. 223 and 230. As it happened Khalil (an army officer until he entered politics) was given a pension instead of an invitation to participate in the military government. Later, he was even imprisoned.

25. B. S. Sharma, "Failure of 'Local Government-Democracy' in the Sudan," Political Studies 15, 1 (February 1967): 63. K.D.D. Henderson notes that the commission set up by Abboud also recommended the suspension of elected members where the "wrong" ones were chosen; *Sudan Republic* (New York: Praeger, 1965), p. 142.

26. *Power in Africa*, pp. 241-242.

27. Henderson, *Sudan Republic*, p. 140.

28. First, *Power in Africa*, pp. 232-238.

29. Henderson, *Sudan Republic*, pp. 137-139; First, *Power in Africa*, pp. 246-248.

30. Robert W. Crawford offers an eyewitness account in "Sudan: The Revolution of October, 1964," Mawazo (Kampala) 1, 2 (December 1967); see also First, *Power in Africa*, pp. 253-260.

31. First, *Power in Africa*, p. 258. At first, the junior officers put forward Colonel Mohammed al-Baghir Mohammed as their candidate for head of state, but he was reluctant to accept the post. When soldiers killed nearly twenty people in one incident during the demonstrations, the resulting anti-army feeling convinced the junior officers to return to the barracks. Ibid., pp. 257, 259. The significance in these maneuverings is that Baghir came to power five years later with Nimeiri and is now

first vice-president of the Sudan. In other words, the coalition between professionals and junior officers contemplated in 1964 became a reality in 1969.

32. These were members of al Ansar, religious followers of the Mahdi. They had been brought to Khartoum to welcome Queen Elizabeth of England then paying a visit, and perhaps to demonstrate in opposition to radical policies of the transitional government. In any event they made their displeasure with the radical government clear. Henderson, *Sudan Republic,* pp. 215-216. This event also carried much significance with the military leaders after the Nimeiri coup, as the Ansar movement was seen as a major opponent of the regime. Thus, it may help to explain the attack by the army on the followers of the Mahdi on Aba Island in March 1970.

33. I am heavily indebted to several conversations with Timothy C. Niblock for my comments on both of these points. His argument is developed in "Aspects of Current Sudanese Politics" (paper delivered to the Seminar on African Politics, Institute of Commonwealth Studies, University of London, June 5, 1974).

34. By February 1974 there were 3,993 village councils, 737 town section councils, 281 nomadic encampment councils, 78 market councils, 15 industrial area councils, 228 rural councils, 90 town councils, 35 subprovince councils, and 10 province executive councils. Many of these presumably exist only on paper at this point.

35. According to Nimeiri's report to the SSU National Congress in January 1974, there were 6,381 basic units, 1,892 branch, 325 district, 34 subprovince, and 10 province organizations. Niblock, "Aspects of Current Sudanese Politics," p. 2.

36. He received the support of 98.6% of the voters—about normal for such elections. Niblock questions whether the ballot was secret. "Aspects," p. 3. The constitution now requires that the SSU nominate a candidate for president who then runs in a national plebescite.

37. These figures are taken from my own research into this election. The SSU did not pass on the suitability of any candidates in this election.

38. This argument is developed in Nelson Kasfir, *The Shrinking Political Arena: Ethnicity and Participation in African Politics* (Berkeley and Los Angeles: University of California Press, 1975).

NELSON KASFIR teaches government at Dartmouth College. He has carried out field research in Uganda and Sudan.

Liberation by *Golpe*

RETROSPECTIVE THOUGHTS ON THE DEMISE OF AUTHORITARIAN RULE IN PORTUGAL

PHILIPPE C. SCHMITTER
University of Chicago

On 25 April 1974, a *golpe de estado* by young officers of the armed forces suddenly and unexpectedly catapulted Portugal into a turbulent and uncertain process of national liberation. In this ironic case, Europe's oldest colonial empire was liberated, not from foreign domination or control, but from forty-eight years of its own authoritarian rule. Whether this movement toward national self-liberation will become a revolution and, if so, what kind is still far from clear. However, whatever the eventual extent of social and economic transformation, the changes in political structure to date have already been irreversible. Reaction and counterrevolution can by no means be ruled out, but should they triumph, the new despots of Portugal will not be able to inherit intact the institutions and practices of Oliveira Salazar or Marcello Caetano, nor will they find it so easy to recapture even the illusory "normality" of that previous pattern of authoritarian rule.

To my knowledge, no scholarly or journalistic observer of Portugal foresaw the overthrow of Marcello Caetano, much less the rapid and complete collapse of authoritarian rule in Portugal. Quite the contrary.

AUTHOR'S NOTE: *The author wishes to thank the Social Sciences Divisional Research fund of the University of Chicago for financial support in connection with this essay, the Committee on Latin American Studies of the University of Chicago for its secretarial assistance. An earlier draft of this essay was presented and discussed at the Mini-Conference on Contemporary Portugal, Yale University, 28-29 May 1975.*

The mini-boom in Portuguese studies of 1972-1973 produced several supposedly objective and documented essays by North American social scientists that emphasized the dynamic, reformist, and presumably viable qualities of the Caetano regime.[1] Marxist and/or radical scholars, despite a more critical scrutiny of the data and their more or less perennial wishful thinking about the imminent maturation of contradictions, also failed to predict the overthrow of Caetano and the extent and profundity of political change that have so far accompanied it.[2] Only the most labored and retrodictive effort could "prove" that objective structural factors "required" the collapse of authoritarian rule in Portugal in 1974 and not before.[3]

Let me hasten to add that my own foresight was no better. I did emphasize in an earlier essay on Portuguese corporatism the imposed and coercive nature of that country's authoritarian regime, the "hollowness" of its structures of interest and partisan representation, the fragility of its social base even among its greatest beneficiaries, and the stalemate of its policy pattern.[4] However, I cannot pretend to have correctly diagnosed its internal cleavages or predicted its imminent demise. During the 1973 Durham Conference on Contemporary Portugal (see note 1), I recall having suggested somewhat hyperbolically—in order to emphasize the severe limitations on Caetano's capacity for accomplishing his stated goal of a "renovation within continuity"—that "Portugal is already a military dictatorship, only no one is aware of it yet." By that, I meant to imply that the military and colonial bureaucracies had put such tight constraints around Caetano's "space for political maneuver" that, for all intents and purposes, they were already governing the country. I was not (in retrospect) wrong about the nature of the severe limitations on guided change imposed by colonial war, imperial economic interests, and ossified political and administrative structures, but I was clearly and emphatically wrong about the direction that political change was about to take—if not about its agents.

Of course, one can fail to foresee (even to conceive of) the likelihood of such a major system transformation simply because of lack of concerted attention to the case in question or misinformation about the facts of the situation. Since there are few scholars or even journalists concertedly interested in Portugal and even fewer reliable public sources of information about political events in that country, the fact that the 25 April coup should have been received as such a surprise should not in itself be so surprising. I could easily plead guilty on both counts, inattention and misinformation, and thereby absolve myself of intellectual blame. However, I am almost certain that, even if I had watched Portugal more closely since finishing my field work there in 1972 and even if my sources of information had been bountiful and reliable, I would *not* have predicted or understood *ex ante* what was about to happen.

The reason for this myopia, I submit, lies primarily in the set of conceptual spectacles through which we have grown accustomed to viewing authoritarian polities. All such lenses—"paradigms," if you will—are of course designed to distort by focusing in an exaggerated manner on those aspects of the political process believed to be most significant, salient, and indicative of future performance. The Portuguese experience since 25 April suggests that our lenses for observing authoritarian rule may already need regrinding, despite the recentness of their acquisition. They seem to have been much better at producing snapshots than motion pictures.

THE AUTHORITARIAN REGIME GESTALT

The specification of a distinctive type or mode of political domination that came to be called authoritarian was undoubtedly a conceptual step forward, one which has proven heuristically useful to a number of scholars working on a large and geographically dispersed set of empirical cases. In our zeal, however, to convince others (and ourselves) that authoritarian regimes were not mere transitory aberrations—neither frustrated totalitarian polities nor nascent polyarchies—we tended to place a great deal of emphasis on their interdependent institutional structures, their mutually compatible behavioral, normative, and ideational properties, their impressive policy flexibility, and, of course, their extraordinary persistence and longevity. Witness the following description:

> In this syndrome, the political process is dominated by a heterogenous elite, itself composed of functionally differentiated bureaucratically organized hierarchic "orders." These encapsulated, non-competitive "orders" have been heavily penetrated by the State. Thus processes of interest representation and leadership selection are controlled from above. Corporatist ideology to the contrary notwithstanding, these orders are not politically equal for the military establishment is frequently (but not always) predominant. Vertical, compartmentalized interactions and exchanges are encouraged; horizontal ones on a class, regional or subcultural basis are discouraged, if not prohibited. The exercise of executive power consists of a deliberate but flexible balancing of these sectoral-functional hierarchies.

The processes of electoral selection and legislative approval are controlled by a single dominant party which neither monopolizes access to influential roles nor enforces rigid ideological conformity. On the contrary, authoritarian regimes deliberately cultivate a multiple legitimacy base—a calculated mixture of traditional, charismatic, legal-rational and technical efficiency principles— and demand of their subjects compliance rather than active support or enthusiasm. This complex, subtle, often contradictory basis of legitimacy distinguishes these regimes from narrowly tyrannical or expedientially dictatorial (and hence, illegitimate) *regimes d'exception*.

The decision-making process is depoliticized and deideologized as far as possible. Emergent problems are converted into legal and administrative issues; challenges to prevailing policies are usually answered by co-optation and selective privilege rather than substantive modification or wholesale repression.[5]

This historically inducted, constructive-ideal type of regime appears, in the above description, *politico-logically* awesome in the way it emphasizes mutually supportive structural properties and coordinately flexible behavioral outcomes. Moreover, it has also proved *empirically* convincing when juxtaposed to the performance of such persistent and stable cases as Portugal, Spain, and Mexico and even rather compelling when applied to such less continuous and shorter-lived examples as Brazil, Egypt, Turkey, and, lately, Peru.[6]

This Gestalt or syndrome of authoritarian rule contains no hint of major contradictory properties, self-defeating tendencies, structural limits to variability and capacity, or even elements of evolutionary transformation—except for a few, almost ad hoc suggestions about shift or alternation between subtypes.[7] Once established, it appears virtually impregnable and invulnerable. Despite both politico-logical and empirical evidence of sclerotic tendencies in long-consolidated authoritarian regimes, very little attention has been paid to their degenerative properties. For example, Juan Linz has argued persuasively that populist-mobilizational varieties of authoritarian rule tend to evolve toward bureaucratic or "organic statist" forms and that totalitarian regimes may also be moving in a similar direction; but he does not even speculate about what follows from this lowest-common-denominator subtype, best exemplified by Portugal and Spain. We are left with the impression that once this Gestalt has been assembled no further regime change is to be anticipated.[8]

THE BONAPARTIST "SITUATION"

As such, the authoritarian regime syndrome was and is purely and calculatedly[9] "political," i.e., divorced from any suppositions about the socioeconomic context from which it arises, from which it extracts needed resources, to which it may be held accountable, for which it distributes benefits (and costs), and upon which it may impose policy-induced transformations. In my work, I have sought to relate this mode of political domination to a particular historical and socioeconomic configuration ("delayed dependent capitalist development") with its attendant structures of property, class, and power relations. Along with others, I found Marx's analysis of the origins of the Second Empire and Engel's comments on Bismarckian Prussia/Germany a very insightful starting point. This, in turn, has led me to focus on what Marx so expressively called *die verselbständigte Machte der Executivgewalt*—the process whereby the state or executive power becomes progressively more autonomous. Hence, to the static descriptive Gestalt of authoritarian rule, I added yet another element of stability—derived from both "external" historical context and "internal" structural properties—the *relative* but significant autonomy of the state (or its executive decisional element) from immediately enforceable accountability to any single social class, faction of class, or even stable alliance (historical bloc) of classes.[10]

By such devices and/or practices as cooptation, patronage, selective concession, change in supportive coalitions, ability to mediate between classes and class factions, cultivation of nationalist symbols, exercise of "judicious" coercion, and so forth, an authoritarian regime could resist capitalist development and modernization or, better, control their political consequences by moving preemptively when and where change seemed unavoidable. The capacity to shift accountability across both time and issue arenas and to exploit superior physical and technical resources seemed to give the state in such a context considerable specific policy flexibility and general structural stability.

Taken to the extreme—i.e., overlooking the qualifying word, "relative"—the authoritarian regime becomes a virtually self-sustaining entity, a cohesive, purposeful, demi-urgic, omnipresent, and omnipotent force that molds civil society to fit the state's reproductive and expansive needs, instead of acting as the responsive agent of societal imperatives as implied by the liberal-democratic scenario or the agent of a revolutionary transformation of productive relations as in the communist-totalitarian situation.

Even where it is demonstrably less than completely self-directive and self-sustaining, the relative autonomy of the state nevertheless serves to protect and insulate the authoritarian regime from the exogenous shocks of the international environment and the endogenous clashes of national classes. Whereas Marx expressed the rather optimistic conviction that Napoleon III could not sustain the non-zero-sum illusion of appearing to benefit all classes at once or maintain his personalistic legitimacy by keeping the public gaze fixed on himself, and, hence, would quickly be defeated by the very heterogeneity and inconsistency of his policies, in studies of Brazil and Portugal I neither expressed nor felt much optimism about the imminent demise of such speculative rule in hothouse fashion. I pointedly remarked that:

> In retrospect Marx was wrong—at least with respect to the time perspective. Napoleon II presided over a sustained economic transformation of France and was finally removed from power twenty years later only by defeat in international war. Since then, developments in political and material technology have made it vastly easier to establish and implement a consistent set of policies, to capture evidence of emerging opposition by social indicators and/or survey research and to act preemptively, to regiment political activity in a single official party, to "corporatize" systems of interest representation, to retain a monopoly over the instruments of organized violence, and to socialize and indoctrinate subjects through the media and mass education.[11]

Again, hindsight makes the defect in conceptual lenses obvious. By stressing the Bonapartist nature of the social roots of authoritarian rule—i.e., the context in which a particularly stalemated, nonhegemonic pattern of class and sectoral relations give rise to a relative autonomy of the state apparatus in both its organizational structure and policy process—they reinforced our tendency to see all forms of immobility as stability and all evidence of persistence as flexibility. They probably caused us to overestimate the degree of relative autonomy of the state and definitely failed to alert us to the limits within which dynamic conservative properties could be sustained in the face of both secular structural trends and episodic conjunctural events.

THE POLITICAL CULTURAL CONGRUENCE

Prior to the emergence of contemporary speculation about the nature of authoritarian rule and/or the revival of interest in Bonapartism, the dominant conceptual framework for explaining the causes and context of nondemocratic rule in Western political systems was some variant of national character or political culture. Held to be the distinctive product of a particular cultural region ("Iberian," "Mediterranean"), authoritarian or Fascist regimes, it was argued, corresponded to a unique configuration of continuous historical experience, intellectual aspirations, elite preferences, and/or popular expectations and values about political life. In this paradigm, cause and effect were somewhat fused, if not confused. Authoritarian regimes were said to emerge or persist because the cultural tradition was "authoritarian, patrimonial, Catholic, stratified, corporate and semi-feudal to the core"; proof that such a cultural tradition was empirically existent and effective rested upon the emergence and persistence of regimes that *were* "authoritarian, patrimonial, Catholic, stratified, corporate and semi-feudal to the core."[12]

I will not develop this line of thought further, partly because it has been exhaustively explored in several recent essays,[13] and partly because my own patent disagreement with its basic assumptions makes me a very ineffectual expositor. However, it is quite clear that this type of speculation is even less capable than the two previous ones of explaining collapse and/or rapid self-transformation. Unless its proponents are prepared to argue that political culture is some sort of "spigot variable" which can be turned on and off (and then explain why and how it gets tightened or loosened), or to argue that such deeply ingrained and historically rooted values are subject to quick reversals of content and form (and then explain what accounts for such a massive changing of minds), they are not likely to contribute much to explaining its effect upon the dynamics of authoritarian rule. One Swiss journalist has put it well: "The Portuguese national temperament has often been described as passive, fatalistic and endlessly melancholy. But anyone travelling through Portugal these days cannot help wondering to what extent this supposed temperament was not imposed and inculcated by 48 years of police-state atmosphere.[14] So far reluctant to invert their causal logic and ask how different regime types can create and manipulate cultural symbols and norms to their advantage, political culturalists find that their interpretive posture now places them defensively in the role of Cassandras, perennially predicting that attempts to move into or along other developmental paths in such inauspicious cultural settings will only result in institutional chaos, anomic confusion, and eventual reversion to "normal" type, and, of course, expecting that such a reaction would belatedly vindicate their earlier inferences.[15]

THE EFFECT OF EXOGENOUS FORCES

The wearers of any or all of our three sets of conceptual spectacles might be excused for their lack of foresight with respect to Portugal if the sudden demise of authoritarian rule there could be shown to be the result of some act of fortune, some unpredictable exogenous process or event that alone can explain the unexpected outcome.

There is, of course, a very tempting candidate for this *deus ex machina:* defeat in war. No one who has written or even speculated about the "Revolution of the 25th of April" can ignore the importance of the influence upon it of the previous regime's conduct of its colonial wars in Africa. The Movimento das Forças Armadas (MFA), the manifest and quite specific agent of its demise, was clearly a product of that exogenous circumstance. Significantly, the MFA's historical origins seem to have come primarily from the Guinée-Bissau theatre where the ecology of the military command structure was unique and where the strategic situation was most immediately hopeless—unlike Angola and Mozambique.[16] In Guinée-Bissau, real military defeat seemed imminent and, owing to the theatre's small size and spatial confinement, interaction among junior officers was particularly intense.[17] General Spínola, who was supreme commander in that theatre from 1969 to 1973, also seems to have drawn his policy conclusions (and made his political alliances) primarily within that context.[18]

Playing the mental counterfactual game, we find that it is indeed difficult to imagine that liberation from established authoritarian rule could have occurred in Portugal without such an external contradiction. This "pessimistic" observation serves to reinforce previous ones based on the Second Empire in France, Wilhelmian Germany, Fascist Italy, and a bevy of Eastern European examples.[19] The contradictions of authoritarian rule would, this suggests, lie outside and beyond the reach of the national civil society in which it is embedded. The only effective praxis of strategy for overthrowing it, then, would be to encourage such a regime to initiate an imperialist war or to defend its existing imperial domain by military means.

This preliminary conclusion does, however, leave a number of questions unanswered:

(1) Why did the authoritarian regime not admit defeat in what was obviously a minor and insignificant part of its imperial domain? Or for that matter, why could it not divest itself of most, if not all, of its colonial possessions, *al la Espanola*, in the interests of metropolitan survival?

(2) Why did "liberation from without" take so long to occur? Why did the persistent strain of thirteen years of colonial war not accomplish this much sooner?

(3) More important, what (if any) prior changes in government structure and performance occurred which may have made the plotters more confident of success? Were not some purely internal transformations necessary prerequisites of an external overthrow?

(4) Why did the coup, once successful, take the policy direction that it did? Why did it so quickly spill over into the civilian sector and result in such a tremendous popular mobilization?

(5) Why was the regime so totally incapable of defending itself? Why was the emperor suddenly revealed to have been so naked?

In short, the counter-counterfactual speculation is equally provocative: Would the coup by a very small group of dissatisfied junior officers[20] have been successful and/or had the repercussions it immediately had, if the previous authoritarian regime had been as structurally coherent, relatively autonomous from societal accountability, and normatively congruent with Portuguese political culture as our previous paradigms led us to believe? The answer to this is, I submit, "No, about as highly unlikely as the coup's having occurred in the absence of impending military defeat."

STRAINS, CLEAVAGES, AND CONTRADICTIONS IN AUTHORITARIAN RULE

Several of the above questions are nearly unanswerable (especially the first). Or, at least, they would require much more extended and detailed treatment than is possible in a speculative essay like this. Let us, therefore, examine briefly certain changes in structural relationships within the Portuguese authoritarian regime and in its relationship to Portuguese society to see if together they can provide us with the beginnings of an answer.

1. The formidable institutional and behavioral interdependence and stability of authoritarian rule are, to a large extent, a temporal illusion. By freezing authoritarian rule's characteristics at one point, the analyst may forget that the historical processes that established such a Gestalt were by no means so synchronized. They involved a great deal of uncertainty, experimentation, failure, coercion, and violence until something like a coherent interdependent institutional pattern emerged. More important, that pattern, once established, is also subject to the inexorable "law of

uneven development."[21] Given the very high sensitivity of such a regime to attaining and sustaining a balance between functionally differentiated, hierarchically structured, privileged orders (the armed forces, civil service, the church, industry, commerce, agriculture, etc.), it must continually cope with and adjust its access and policy patterns to the differential effect of such generic processes as economic growth, urbanization, inflation, changes in the terms and volume of foreign trade, technological innovation, emigration, demographic increase, inflows of foreign capital, evolution of wage structures, secularization, and so forth. Part of the "secret" of Portuguese stability, no doubt, lay in the relatively slow and even rates of change in these potentially destabilizing, "desynchronizing" developmental variables (an outcome itself in large measure the product of deliberate policy). Portugal throughout the 1930s and well into the 1950s had the lowest rates of urbanization, improvement in literacy, industrialization, and general economic modernization of any European country. However, during the 1960s many of these began to accelerate, especially those with ambiguous and highly differentiated effects: economic growth, emigration, inflation, and inflows of foreign capital.

The very success of *Estado Novo* institutions in coping with the earlier period of slower and more controlled change (aided initially by the special circumstances of wartime emergency and international isolation) led to ossification and inability to deroutinize their activities in the face of new claimants and new demands. Nowhere was this more evident than in the corporative complex of state-sponsored interest associations and state-controlled sectoral policy-making agencies.[22] Attempts to reform or reinvigorate these institutions failed miserably, as did similarly half-hearted efforts with respect to the government party, the planning apparatus, and public administration as a whole.

2. Nevertheless, despite the accelerating and differential effect of social and economic change in the 1960s, on the one hand, and institutional and policy ossification, on the other, there is nothing in the period immediately preceding the April coup to suggest imminent collapse or even acute difficulties of these environmental-structural grounds alone. In fact, the short-term aggregate performance of the regime and of the Portuguese economy was, if anything, relatively impressive in 1972 and 1973. With the exception of the skyrocketing rate of emigration (itself a safety valve for popular dissatisfaction and an important source of foreign exchange to compensate for an increasing deficit in foreign trade), none of the items in Table 1 show dramatically disproportionate increases or provide evidence for a particularly critical conjuncture. By Western

TABLE 1
Aggregate Indicators of Economic Performance: 1960-1973

	1960	1961	1962	1963	1964	1965	1966	1967	1968	1969	1970	1971	1972	1973
Total GNP	100	107	115	125	138	151	168	186	203	224	252	292	302
Total Governmental Expenditures	100	110	117	128	134	146	174	187	206	236	238	304	324*
Total Military Expenditures	100	116	119	134	151	165	199	218	230	252	219	235	266*
Consumer Prices (Lisbon)	100	103	105	108	113	118	125	133	144	154	172	189	215
Wages in Industry (Lisbon)	100	106	112	118	125	134	146	158	176	198	218	237	265
Wages in Agriculture	100	119	125	140	149	174	191	228	245	276	318	356	402
Industrial Production	100	100	104	114	119	125	123	130	142	149	160	179	169
Emigration (Net Annual Outflow)	100	117	159	228	287	322	262	259	468	571	505	351	401
Total Imports	100	89	100	118	141	156	161	180	198	241	278	340	408
Total Exports	100	113	128	158	177	190	215	233	262	291	323	397	596
Gold and Foreign Reserves	100	121	128	153	165	189	216	239	253	263	342	403	447

SOURCES: OECD, *Economic Survey, Portugal*, various issues; Bank of London & South America, *Review* (September 1974); Banco Nacional Ultramarino, *Boletin Trimestral*, No. 97 (January-March 1974); A. Proença Varão, "Sistema Econômico e Política Regional," *Seará Nova*, No. 1535 (September 1973).
*budgeted

European standards for the period, the comparative performance was poor—but evenly so.

While a good deal has been justifiably written about the way in which the mode of political domination in Portugal was impeding the development of capitalist productive forces and about the emergence of important structural bottlenecks in the balance of payments, capital accumulation, agricultural production, import substitution industrialization, and adaptation to European competition, nothing I can find "proves" that these "reproductive imperatives of capitalism" had reached such a critical stage that a rupture had become "historically necessary." On the contrary, despite the persistent strains of enormous military expenditures, stagnant agricultural production, widening imbalance in the foreign trade account, and the more episodic stresses of the petroleum crisis and decline in tourism, the Caetano regime seemed to be muddling along in its usual cautious and indecisive manner. GNP was still growing; employment was rising; wages, especially in the agricultural sector, seem to have been increasing;[23] international reserves were at an all-time high; receipts from emigrants were coming in greater and greater quantities;[24] the stock market was booming; government revenues had gone up to 19.3% of GNP in 1973 and were budgeted to increase by 22% in 1974; military expenditures were still increasing in absolute terms but decreasing as a proportion of total government expenditures (if the 1974 budget can be trusted in this matter).[25]

To this admittedly incompletely informed observer, these are not the indicators of impending structural collapse, of rapidly ripening "objective" contradictions between the state and civil society. Poor comparative performance, gross and growing inequality, incapacity to modify political structures or to take bold policy initiatives—yes, but these have long been features of Portuguese society and polity. There are no data I know of that show any marked worsening of these unfortunate constants. If anything, the recent Portuguese experience strengthens the old adage that sudden and discontinuous political change is more likely to occur after periods of marked improvement in material conditions of life.

3. Leaving aside for the moment the changing constraints placed on the Portuguese regime by the performance of its national production system and its place in the international political economy, let us turn to another form of linkage between civil society and the state: sense of allegiance to or support for the regime by its subjects-cum-citizens. Apologists for the regime and some political culturalists to the contrary notwithstanding, virtually no objective observer has claimed that the

TABLE 2
Budgeted Military Expenditures As Percentage of
Total Central Government Budgeted Expenditures

Year	%	Absolute Amounts*
1938	22.4	514
1960		
1961	36.5	4907
1962	38.5	5710
1963	37.3	5853
1964	38.3	6552
1965	40.9	7390
1966	41.3	8100
1967	41.9	9785
1968	42.4	10696
1969	40.7	11292
1970	38.9	12346
1971	36.5	10760
1972	33.4	11550
1973	30.0	13070
1974	27.6	14630

SOURCES: *Anvário Estatístico,* various issues; OECD, *Economic Survey: Portugal,* various issues.
*In million escudos.

Salazar-Caetano regime was in any sense popular. In a mass national survey conducted in 1973,[26] 0.9% reported that *the* national aspect of which they were most proud was its "sistema político." However, 7.4% expressed most pride in "the government and authorities," 1.2% in "the armed forces," and 0.0% in national legislative deputies (deputados).[27] The results of this—unfortunately, "one-shot"—survey hardly confirm our belief in the "naturalness" or "cultural congruence" of the regime and also tell us nothing about its evolution over time.

For various reasons, authoritarian regimes are likely to show a steady decline in citizen-subject allegiance over time (never having departed from very high levels in the first place). The deliberate cultivation of compliance rather than enthusiasm; the use of intermediary associations for social control rather than political mobilization; the inability of their anti-utopian, "realistic" ideology to compete with the attractions of such utopian and widely disseminated *Weltanschauung* as liberalism, socialism, and communism; the declining marginal returns from repeated appeals to patriotism, national heritage, external enemies, etc.; the sheer complacency of men who have been in power so long—all conspire to make it especially difficult for such regimes to retain the active allegiance of their supporters and beneficiaries during the course of their political careers, and even more difficult for them to transmit such supportive values across generations.

In the complete absence of any reliable, longitudinal data on this subject, we can create a tentative simulation of regime support using Markov chain logic and a modest set of axiomatic propositions and specific historical assumptions. By running these out over time from an initial (1930) estimate of the relative proportions of different types of regime supporters and opponents, we can get a crude estimate of how this secular trend toward disaffection evolved in Portugal.

We can divide the Portuguese adult male population into five types of support groups: (1) active enthusiasts, (2) passive supporters, (3) semi opponents, (4) active opponents, and (5) excluded apathetics.[28] We can assume differential shifts in the behavior of those adults already actively or passively engaged in politics and differential recruitment of their sons to political life. Then, "guesstimating" the initial (ca. 1930) distribution of the population in regime support, we can simulate the pattern of decline in allegiance over time.[29]

These proportional figures for the five categories of regime support are manifestly and deliberately fictitious and have yet to be sensitivity-tested to determine how they fluctuate with different estimates of original distribution or different assumptions about intergenerational change. However, they do suggest an interesting observation. While support does decline and opposition does increase monotonically because of "imperfections" in the intergenerational transmission of allegiance (as well as some defection among adult activists), its pattern is curvilinear with a clear tendency toward deceleration rather than acceleration. Relatively large proportional shifts would have occurred during the first thirty years of the regime. Later, a sort of unpopular stabilization occurs. Enthusiasm continues to decline (but less so, since given small proportional cooptations of passive supporters will suffice to compensate for disaffection in what was already a small group of enthusiasts). However, passive support and apathy provide a large and relatively constant "pad" or cushion between those in power and their militant opponents. If one used a crude, minimal winning opposition majority notion (i.e., semi-opponents + active opponents = 51%) to determine the point at which an entrenched authoritarian regime could become critically vulnerable, this would only have reached 33.5% by 1990 according to assumptions of this model, and

TABLE 3
Simulated Patterns of Support for Authoritarian Rule:
1930-1990

	1930 Estimate	1945 Simulation	1960 Simulation	1975 Simulation	1990 Simulation
Active enthusiasts	10.0%	8.3%	7.2%	6.4%	5.7%
Passive supporters	30.0	29.2	29.0	28.7	29.2
Semi-opponents	10.0	12.7	14.2	15.3	15.9
Active opponents	10.0	13.0	15.0	16.6	17.6
Excluded apathetics	40.0	36.8	34.6	33.0	31.6
	100.0	100.0	100.0	100.0	100.0

was only about 32% in 1974. By this *ceteribus paribus* politico-logic, the Caetano regime was not threatened by an active civilian, mass opposition; it was still protected by an ample pad of passivity and apathy.

To provide greater historical realism for this exercise in heuristic simulation, I have recalculated regime support, modifying the coefficients for each category to account for three very important structural changes occurring after 1960: (1) accelerated urbanization and industrialization (primarily acting to decrease probable apathy); (2) massive emigration (having an inverse effect); and (3) colonial war and protracted military service (depressing regime support by reducing the intergeneration transmission of favorable allegiance among draft-eligible sons of supporters and by increasing more active forms of opposition). The revised simulated outcomes are presented in Table 4.

On a net basis, the post-1960 structural changes definitely accelerated regime disaffection by increasing opposition (mostly, however, among the passive semi-opponents) and, more dramatically, by cutting sharply into the proportion of passive supporters. This had in the past played a crucial role, amortizing the shocks between enthusiasts and militant opponents and providing a cooptable mass to replenish the continuously depleted ranks of regime enthusiasts. The proportional importance of apathy appeared to have increased after 1960, mainly owing to massive emigration.

Any such exercise in the simulation of regime support is, of course, primarily a sort of intellectual game. No matter how "reasonable" its axiomatic assumptions and how "correct" its basic theorems about the secular tendency for intergenerational allegiance to decline in authoritarian

TABLE 4
Revised Simulated Patterns of Support for Authoritarian Rule: 1930-1990

	1930 Estimate	1945 Simulation	1960 Simulation	1975 Rev. Simulation	1990 Rev. Simulation
Active enthusiasts	10.0%	8.3%	7.2%	5.9%	4.7%
Passive supporters	30.0	29.2	29.0	25.1	21.7
Semi-opponents	10.0	12.7	14.2	17.6	19.4
Active opponents	10.0	13.0	15.0	16.9	19.1
Excluded apathetics	40.0	36.8	34.6	34.4	34.9
	100.0	100.0	100.0	99.9	99.8

regimes,[30] it can never constitute any sort of a "proof" that the Caetano regime was viable in terms of mass support—i.e., not yet vulnerable to widespread citizen disaffection. Opposition to a regime is not only related to many immediate and conjunctural factors, above and beyond secular and structural trends, but is also dependent on the distribution of existing disaffection by class, sector, and region. Nevertheless, all these caveats aside, the politico-logic of the simulation exercise does strongly suggest that accumulated mass disaffection is not likely, as long as substantial apathy persists or a proportionally large group of passive supporters survives, to threaten the viability of authoritarian rule. This form of political domination, especially in its demobilized, bureaucratized, exclusionist subtype, does not depend on enthusiasm. It cultivates and survives because of passive opportunism and apathy; and neither of these qualities seems to have diminished markedly in the period preceding the regime's overthrow in April 1974.

4. The above explorations lead to the empirical conclusion—indeed, to the tentative theoretical generalization—that *the sources of contradiction, necessary if not sufficient for the overthrow of authoritarian rule, lie within the regime itself, within the apparatus of the state, not outside it in its relations with civil society.* The Portuguese example seems to demonstrate that authoritarian regimes have more to fear from their apparent supporters than from their manifest opponents.[31] Also, it suggests that, when the crunch is on, the greatest beneficiaries and most privileged elements of the regime will be unable or unwilling to rise to its defense. "Objective" constraints and "subjective" opponents may create

and/or articulate the persistent strains and episodic pressures that exacerbate internal cleavages, upset delicate balances between established hierarchical orders, weaken the resolve of regime supporters to act, and decrease the viability of certain preemptive and repressive policy options. However, alone, without such prior "reflexive" changes within the governing apparatus itself, they are not likely to be sufficient to threaten the regime, much less overthrow it.

Another way of expressing the nature of its vulnerability is to suggest that the contradictions of authoritarian rule are peculiarly political and administrative—more closely linked to the *forms* in which state power is organized, the *distributional effect* of policy on agents of the state, and the means whereby state authority is transferred from one set of supporters to another. The contradictions of liberal-democratic political domination lie primarily in the public arenas of class, sectoral and regional group conflict, electoral competition and mobilization, and the societal influence of policy change and shifts in public opinion. Those of authoritarian polities are a good deal less visible—but none the less real.[32] To monitor them we need to pay attention to behaviors which are rather different and no doubt much more difficult to measure.

To suggest that "intestinal contradictions" exist, of course, tells us nothing about what and where "these worms in the entrails of the body politic" in fact are. The following are a few tentative suggestions about what the structural basis of these cleavages may be, based on illuminative hindsight of the Portuguese case, that I think could be argued to have offered a sort of archetype of demobilized, exclusionist, bureaucratic, authoritarian rule.

The most generic form of cleavage within such regimes lies in the relationships between institutionalized "orders" of special privilege and status. Usually these hierarchic "pillars" of authoritarian rule have historical origins which antedate the regime itself (e.g., the church, the army, the civil service, local notables) that after some purging or pruning are coopted and built into the emergent governing system on the basis of a quid pro quo involving relative sectoral or professional autonomy in exchange for interest specialization, compartmentalized demand, and controls over leadership selection. Sometimes, especially where the consolidation of authoritarian rule succeeds a revolution or civil war, the state may have to create representative structures *de novo,* e.g., a single governmental party or a corporatist interest system, in order to displace existing ones or to fill empty political space.

The relationships between such pillars are not necessarily fixed over time, nor are their number and identity. A successful authoritarian regime will be able to modify the terms of relative exchange, access, and advantage, and even may admit whole new sets of actors to the game. In short, this form of political domination may change by a process of sedimentation and shifting, usually punctuated by major cabinet shuffles or evidenced by the creation of new intersectoral agencies or even ministries. A clue to the special structural weakness of the Portuguese system was its extraordinary dependence on the discretion of a single individual under Salazar, the almost complete absence of any cabinet-level process of intersectoral consultation and deliberation, the considerable ambiguity (after Salazar's removal from office and death in 1968) in the respective roles of the President of the Republic and the President of the Council,[33] the rigidity of ministerial roles and competences and the extreme importance that financial or fiscal considerations and controls had within the apparatus of the state. Marcello Caetano was a compromise product who inherited a very brittle and delicately balanced decisional structure that he never succeeded in either dominating or modifying.[34] The failure of his (admittedly not very vigorous or concerted) attempts to build in young technocratic elements, to create new interministerial agencies, and to introduce cabinet-level collective deliberation were evidence of this, along with the rather resounding failure of his reputedly more innovative ministers to resuscitate or reform their specific policy domains.[35]

Two pairs of relationships within the authoritarian state appear to be particularly crucial: church-state and civil-military.

The degeneration of the first has been extensively and excellently treated in a recent monograph,[36] so little needs to be added. Here the obvious structural problem lies in the special external linkages of ecclesiastic authority and ideological diffusion that resulted both in a growing internal fragmentation of this legitimating pillar of the regime and the widening estrangement, even opposition, of some of its members not just to the occupants of secular authority roles but to the authoritarian form of political domination itself.

But this contradiction was only a minor irritation compared to that which developed between civilian authorities and the military. In the complete absence of scholarly monographs or even good journalistic descriptions of the Portuguese military, we are left with fleeting glimpses and speculative inferences about how and why this fissure developed.

First, it is important to note that since roughly 1930 the Portuguese regime was not, de jure or de facto, a military dictatorship. The military saviors of 1926 gave way, in form and in content, to a civilian who, while he continued to devote a substantial proportion of government revenues to military expenditures (+25%), definitely enforced an institutional separation between civilian and military authority with the former predominant. The only important residue lay in the calculated selection by Salazar of senior military officers to become honorific presidents of the republic.[37]

Second, however, civil-military relations have never been so historically pacific and orderly as the regime's overall record of stability could have led one to believe. Substantial numbers of military officers were involuntarily retired in the early 1930s and there were periodic garrison-type revolts in 1927, 1931, 1935, 1936, 1946, 1947, 1951, 1959, and as late as 1961 in Beja. Quixotic as many of these were, they undoubtedly left a residue of frustrated careers, clique networks, and heroic images within the military establishment and a set of personal contacts with civilian opposition groups who participated, however ineffectually, in almost every one of these attempts.[38]

Third, the treatment of the defeated garrison in Goa revealed the unrealistic and external nature of Salazar's command over the army. It taught many officers that the armed forces as an institution and perhaps they as individual officers could become the public scapegoats in the event of another such defeat. Incidents in Beira, Mozambique in January 1974—where Portuguese colonials insulted soldiers and officers in the streets for not pursuing the war vigorously enough—no doubt reinforced the lesson.[39]

Fourth, even prior to the outbreak of colonial wars in 1961, recruitment patterns to the army officer corps were dramatically altered when Salazar in 1958 removed all tuition charges from the Military Academy and offered salaries to cadets for the first time. Predictably, this produced a sudden influx of middle-class and petit bourgeois entrants. Presumably this meant that incoming cadets came from families with no previous connections with the military, and little or no economic measures to supplement the meager pay and semi-professional status of the Portuguese armed forces. The class of 1962, the first enlisted under the new system, graduated just in time to provide officers for the most exposed combat roles and repeated tours of duty in the fighting in Guinée, Mozambique, and Angola. Most of the "captains" of April 1974 came from this "discontinuous" cohort of professional army officers.[40]

Fifth, the protractedness of the colonial wars plus the modest demographic size of Portugal led to massive and concentrated conscription of troops and, especially, of junior officers.[41] Recruiting junior officers directly from university faculties, where opposition to the regime was most intensive, could, one may suspect, have introduced the fatal flaw into the command structure.

This was, indeed, the case—but only by paradox or dialectical reaction. The organizers of the MFA seem to have all come from the *regular,* not conscript, officer corps. In fact, their initial impetus for forming in July 1973 seems to have come in reaction to a Defense Ministry decree permitting university-recruited conscript officers *(milicianos)* entry and promotion rights equivalent to those of officers who passed through the normal, full training circuit and transforming the former four year course of the Military Academy into a two-semester one. This "ridiculization" of the educational experience and loss of professional status of a new group of officers already distinguished by their lower social origins and higher mobility aspirations was "the drop that made the chalice overflow, since there was already a great degree of discontent among the permanent officer corps who could not see a military solution to the war as it was developing in Africa."[42]

According to another source, this conspiratorial group informed the draftee officers that they intended to seize power only on the very night they moved. "They came to us and asked if we wanted to join in ... and assured us that it would be no sell-out in Africa and so forth. What they didn't know was that of the six of us, there were two Socialists, one Communist, one Catholic radical, one Trotskyist and one a Cape Verdian who supported the PAIGC."[43] The changing pattern of junior officer recruitment and the internal conflict within their ranks help explain *dialectically* how professional and status motivations lay at the origin of the attempt to seize power and *additively* why, once its members had moved to seize power, the MFA was able so quickly to expand its ranks and consolidate its victory.

Finally, and most important, this *excursis* into microelements of military sociology fails to tell us why such initially minor complaints were compounded into a threat to the nature of political domination itself. Why could this not have been corporatistically encapsulated and resolved by some sort of compromise? Clearly, the deteriorating military situation and the sheer necessity for more junior officers, coupled with other complaints, such as forced and rapid rotations back into combat, played a role—but equally if not more important was the growing factional split at the top of the Portuguese military establishment. The right-wing, procolonial officers and their civilian allies failed by a narrow margin in December 1973 to have Caetano removed as President of the Council because of the indecision or opposition of Admiral Thomaz, who, as President of the Republic, had the formal (but never exercised) authority to remove him. Caetano then found that he had to create a more viable support base. Completely unable to do this through the mobilization of any civilian "representative institutions" (for example, the moribund official party), he had to turn to an opposing military faction of doves in the upper levels of the armed forces. The result was encouragement and permission to publish General Antonio de Spínola's book, *Portugal and Its Future,* thereby accelerating a process of fractionalization of power, frantic changes in the top military command structure, and eventually a victorious (but brief) alliance between various insurrectionally inclined levels of the military hierarchy that found in Spínola their temporary symbolic leader.[44]

It is important to note the way in which this primary set of contradictions within the Portuguese state was reinforced by a secondary one: the problem of succession. There were indications of difficulty with the reelection of Admiral Américo Thomaz to the presidency in 1972. Tradition or prudence seems to have established that this office was to rotate among the three military services; army, air force, and navy. A deadlock seems to have ensued; the army was "deprived" of its "rightful" turn.[45]

Marcello Caetano's succession as President of the Council seems to have gone smoothly, although there was a ten-day period of hesitation—perhaps owing to doubts about Salazar's capacity to recuperate. In retrospect, we can now see that Caetano seems to have inherited more of the form than the content of power from his more charismatic predecessor. Although I have not yet read them, I suspect that one of the major themes of Caetano's forthcoming memoirs is likely to be the incomplete manner in which authority was transferred to him and the severe limits placed on his capacity to rule by the peculiarly bicephalic Portuguese executive arrangement.

Unless authoritarian regimes can create a viable, aggregative governmental party that provides an institutional cover for executive succession or, much more problematically, rely upon some parallel form of legitimacy such as the monarchy (Spain), they are likely to find it exceedingly difficult to choose a successor from within their ranks (even when he has been anointed by his outgoing predecessor—as Caetano was not). Above all, it will be difficult for the incumbent to reassert the sort of centralized moderating role that such an office demands. Ironically, precisely because of the ambiguity surrounding his selection and his need to appeal beyond regime enthusiasts to consolidate his hold on office, the incumbent authoritarian ruler may succeed in temporarily disarming some of his opponents—who will at least initially concede him the benefit of the doubt.[46] Therefore, the immediate transfer of formal authority may appear deceptively calm. Only later are the limitations on the ruler's capacity to "renovate within continuity" (to use Caetano's slogan) likely to lead to even higher levels of disillusionment.

A final set of generic internal contradictions appears not to have played a direct part in the overthrow of the former Portuguese regime but helps explain why it was so totally incapable of defending itself. Contemporary authoritarian regimes no longer benefit from the aura of popularity and historical inevitability that once accompanied fascism and gave Fascist regimes a sort of legitimate image as bearers of change in the 1920s and 1930s. Also gradually declining in legitimizing efficency, as we have seen, has been the appeal to unique national tradition and the longing for order. To compensate for change in historical context and temporal slackening *(afrouxamento)*, this type of regime has increasingly turned to appeals based on economic efficiency and social policy performance. An illustration of this attempt to switch the basis of regime legitimacy was provided by Caetano's decision to discard the label, "O Estado Corporativo," inherited from the 1930s and to call his "reformist" regime "O Estado Social."

Not only does this gradual shift in emphasis increase the regime's vulnerability when it subsequently fails to meet stated performance goals or, even worse, falls steadily behind the performance of referential societies (e.g., Spain and the rest of Europe for Portugal); it also serves to create and legitimate a new set of roles within the state apparatus filled by younger, better-trained occupants often known generically as *técnicos* or technocrats. Willing (at least initially) to overlook or ignore certain less savory aspects of the regime, they introduce new kinds of professional norms, new criteria of rational performance, even some new sets of substantive and procedural goals, within the bureaucracy. Often these orientations are confined to specific technical agencies of the state, but they tend to affect other more clientelistic and particularistic policy sectors as well. They tend to propagate new types of linkages with and expectations among sectors of the propertied classes, especially more modernized sectors of industry, commerce, and agriculture.[47]

In Portugal, the *técnicos'* commitment to development and rationalized use of state resources was severely frustrated by the limited availability of resources owing to war expenditures, as well as by the resistance of traditional bureaucratic elements and their surrounding economic and social clienteles. Their growing awareness of their decisional impotence and their feeling that Portugal was missing out on the crucial external opportunities that European economic integration might have provided drove most of them to resign (or sometimes to be dismissed). It is not difficult to imagine that, as these young, often talented, and ambitious men took up positions in the private sector, they contributed to propagating the belief in such circles that the Portuguese state was incapable of self-regeneration and, hence, incapable in the long run of assuring the reproductive needs of Portuguese capitalism. While there is no evidence that these *técnicos* or more enlightened sectors of the Portuguese bourgeoisie played a direct role in overthrowing the regime,[48] there is also no evidence of the contrary—that they made any effort to defend it.[49]

CONCLUSION

The coup of 25 April 1974 can indeed be described as an inverted national liberation movement, the product of a sort of domino effect working in reverse. An imperial power sought to prevent the serial loss of its colonial overseas dependencies and was itself progressively undermined and then suddenly overthrown by the effort.

Nevertheless, the conspiracy might never have occurred had civil-military relations been differently structured and managed. It might never have been successful had it not been for the regime's incapacity to rally its supporters and beneficiaries. It might never have had the enormous and irreversible political repercussions it has had, had it not been for a pervasive crisis in the state's relation to Portuguese civil society.

Such tentative observations lead us to conclude that existing paradigms for the study of authoritarian modes of political dominance are essentially static. They must be modified to reflect the historically disrhythmic or asynchronic nature of internal contradictions between an authoritarian regime's component hierarchic structures and to explain the conditions under which the relative autonomy of the state may become more a source of weakness than of strength. These paradigms must also divest themselves as much as possible of unwarranted, circular assumptions about the natural congruence between such regimes and their respective national political cultures.

NOTES

1. On 10-14 October 1973, the Council on European Studies sponsored an interdisciplinary Conference/Workshop on Modern Portugal at the University of New Hampshire, Durham, N.H. About 25 scholars from the United States, Great Britain, and Portugal attended. Three of the papers presented there by North Americans expressed considerable optimism about the Caetano regime: Lawrence Graham, "Portugal: The Bureaucracy of Empire"; Henry H. Keith, "Point, Counterpoint in Reforming Portuguese Education: 1750-1973"; and Howard J. Wiarda, "The Portuguese Corporative System: Basic Structures and Current Functions."

2. See, for example, the articles which appeared in Nos. 1-4 of Polémica, a journal published by exiled Marxist social scientists in Geneva. Of particular interest are the articles by Manuel de Lucena.

3. For independent but compatible arguments that the 1974 Revolucão was somehow retrodictively necessary, see Robin Blackburn, "The Test in Portugal," New Left Review, Nos. 87-88 (Sept.-Dec. 1974): 5-48, and Peter McDonough, "Structural Factors in the Decline and Fall of Portuguese Corporatism," paper presented to the Mini-Conference on Modern Portugal, Yale University (28-29 March 1975).

4. "Corporatist Interest Representation and Public Policy-Making in Portugal," paper presented at the Workshop on Modern Portugal, 10-14 October 1973. A revised version of this entitled, "Corporatism and Public Policy in Authoritarian Portugal," will appear shortly in the Sage Publications series on political sociology.

5. "Paths to Political Development in Latin America," in *Changing Latin America*, edited by D. Chalmers (New York: The Academy of Political Science, Columbia University, 1972), pp. 91-92.

6. The Gestalt was initially inducted from the Spanish case and received its "classic" expression in Juan Linz, "An Authoritarian Regime: Spain," in Mass Politics, edited by E. Allardt and S. Rokkan (New York: The Free Press, 1970), pp. 251-283. Linz has recently extended his thoughts to cover a much wider set of cases and suggested several subtypes of authoritarian rule. "Notes toward a Typology of Authoritarian Regimes," paper presented at APSA Congress, Washington, D.C., 5-9 September 1972. For a useful review of the burgeoning literature on this subject, consult Susan Kaufman Purcell, "Authoritarianism," in Comparative Politics 5 (January 1973).

7. In the concluding chapter of my *Interest Conflict and Political Change in Brazil* (Stanford: Stanford University Press, 1971), I discussed the possibility and probable consequences of alternation between "semi-competitive, populist" and "repressive, bureaucratic militarist" subtypes of authoritarian rule.

8. See his "Totalitarian and Authoritarian Regimes," N. Polsby, ed., *Handbook of Political Science* (Reading, Mass.: Addison Wesley, forthcoming).

9. "A pitfall that we should, in my opinion, avoid is to search for a typology of political systems that would include elements of a typology of societies and economic systems," Ibid., p. 5.

10. "The Portugalization of Brazil?" in Alfred Stepan III, ed., *Authoritarian Brazil* (New Haven: Yale University Press, 1973), pp. 179-232, and works cited therein, esp. in footnote 6. Also consult the article by Fernando H. Cardoso, "Associated Dependent Development: Theoretical and Practical Considerations," in the same volume, pp. 142-178.

11. "The Portugalization of Brazil?", p. 190.

12. The quoted expressions are taken from Howard J. Wiarda, "Toward a Framework for the Study of Political Change in the Iberian Latin Tradition," World Politics 25 (January 1973): 106-135.

13. Several of these are conveniently collected in Howard J. Wiarda, ed., *Politics and Social Change in Latin America: The Distinct Tradition* (Amherst: University of Massachusetts Press, 1974). Also see articles by Wiarda, Newton and Pike in T. Stichton and F. Pike, eds., *The New Corporatism* (South Bend, Ind.: Notre Dame University Press, 1974).

14. Arnold Hottinger, "The Dam Breaks in Portugal," Swiss Review of World Affairs 24 (July 1974): 7.

15. These "cataclysmic" implications for the future of Portugal are traced in Howard J. Wiarda, "Prospects for Portugal," unpublished manuscript, 16 October 1974.

16. For a contrary evaluation that the military situation in Mozambique was most hopeless and precipitated the coup, see Robin Blackburn, "Test," p. 6. The new regime's first negotiations to end the colonial war were engaged with PAIGC representing Guinée and the Cabo Verde islands.

17. On the origins of the MFA, see the interview with Otelo Saraiva de Carvalho, "MFA—do nascimento a vitoria final," Expresso (27 July 1974): 17-19. Also Diario de Noticias (29 October 1974) for another interview with a key participant.

18. "Portugal: Kolonien auf Zeit?" Der Spiegel 33 (1973); "Guinée–Bissau: un an après l'assasinat d'Amilcar Cabral," Le Monde (19 January 1974); "A Basically Losing Battle," Newsweek, 6 May 1974; "The General with a Monocle," Newsweek, 6 May 1974; "Un Croisé passionné et résolu," Le Monde (16 May 1974); and, of course, Antonio de Spínola, *Portugal e o Futuro* (Lisbon: Verba, 1974).

19. "The interchanges between the international security environment and political systems would seem to have been the most powerful exogenous variable in explaining system stability and change," Gabriel Almond in G. Almond et al., *Crisis, Choice and Change* (Boston: Little, Brown and Co., 1973), p. 628.

20. Apparently fewer than 150 junior officers participated in the planning and execution of the 25 April coup. The total number of officers in the Portuguese armed forces was over 5,000 at the time. See Otelo Saraiva de Carvalho, "MFA" for details of MFA's initial organization and plotting.

21. The temporally asynchronic nature of authoritarian consolidations of state power is noted by Juan Linz in his "Totalitarian and Authoritarian Regimes," p. 153ff., but not developed further as a source on continuous contradiction and weakness. "Dissynchronization" is also a key concept in G. Almond et al., *Crisis, Choice and Change*, p. 47ff.

22. See Philippe Schmitter, "Corporatist Interest Representation and Public Policy-Making in Portugal," and, to the contrary, Howard J. Wiarda, "The Portuguese Corporative System."

23. Ribeiro de Carvalho, "Salário mínimo e despedimentos," Seará Nova, No. 1548 (October 1974): 9; "Evolução da situação socio-econômica da familias portuguesas (1969-1971)," Seará Nova, No. 1532 (June 1973): 7-8.

24. "Portugal: as remesas dos emigrantes na balança de pagamentos da Metrópole," Análise Social, No. 38 (1973): 381.

25. Not to exaggerate the picture, one should point to a series of indicators of an economic downturn in the later quarter of 1973 and the first quarter of 1974, as the general conjunctural crisis of capitalism and the rise in oil prices began to affect Portugal. Inflation picked up sharply; the stock market boom weakened; agricultural output fell; the rate of industrial production increase declined; tourism was off. For an excellent resume, see OECD, *Economic Survey, Portugal* (1974). This "afrouxamento" in the months immediately preceding the coup is also discussed in Expresso (29 June 1974): 14; also Virgilio Delemos, "L'action des capitaines et l'imagination de la rue," Le Monde Diplomatique (August 1973).

26. *Os Portugueses e a Política–1973,* Estudos IPOPE (Lisbon: Moraes, 1973). This national poll on political attitudes could provide important base line data for later behavioral changes but is vitiated by a rather unrepresentative sample which grossly overrepresents housewives. The published version contains only marginals and a few cross-tabulations.

27. Ibid., p. 59. This same survey from the fall of 1973 also revealed considerable feelings of personal economic progress over the past five years and high expectations about future performance.

28. For a discussion of opposition to authoritarian rule that draws slightly different distinctions than those used here, see Juan Linz, "L'opposizione in un regime autoritario: il case della Spagna," Storia contemporanea 1 (March 1970): 63-104.

29. Readers who wish to obtain the specific intra- and intergenerational estimates upon which this simulation is based are invited to request them from the author. For the general logic of this sort of Markov chain model, see Philip Converse, "Of Time and Partisan Stability," Comparative Political Studies II (1969): 139-71, where it is used to predict increased partisan identification over time.

30. Juan Linz, for example, has proposed a "third generation" law of defection from authoritarian regimes in his "Totalitarian and Authoritarian Regimes," p. 141.

31. After running these initial and corrected simulations of citizen disaffection, I discovered a possible source of independent confirmation of their accuracy. The survey cited in notes 26 and 27 asked its respondents whether they approved of the regime's performance on some fifteen issues. If we consider that those who expressed approval are equivalent to the sum of our simulated "enthusiasts" and "passive supporters," those who disapproved are equivalent to our "opponents" plus "semi-opponents," and those giving no answer are the same as our simulated "apathetics," we arrive at the contrasts shown in Table A. The basic divergence between the "artifacts" of the survey and the "pseudofacts" of the simulation rests in the much greater proportion of nonrespondents-cum-apathetics. If we explain this in part by the biased nature of the sample (i.e., a very high proportion of housewives and women in general) and by the possibility that many who hesitated to express an opinion were, in fact, hiding a disapproving one, the "fit" between the two estimates is not so bad.

TABLE A

Simulation (1974)	Enthusiasts and Passive Supporters	Opponents and Semi-opponents	Apathetics
Original	36	31	33
Corrected	32	34	34
Survey (1973)	Approve	Disapprove	No Answer
All questions (15)	30	21	49
Public welfare issues (4)	33	23	44
Salaries and employment (3)	26	32	42
Political issues (4)	22	24	54
International issues (4)	37	8	55

SOURCE: IPOPE, p. 94.

32. This point is not original. Juan Linz has said much the same thing in his massive "Totalitarian and Authoritarian Regimes," essay.

33. For a list of unobtrusive monitors of authoritarian regime performance, see my "Paths to Political Development in Latin America," pp. 103-5.

34. For a formal-length description of this bicephalism, consult Francisco I. Pereira dos Santos, *Un Etat Corporatif, La Constitution Sociale et Politique Portugaise* (Paris: Sirey, 1940), and Marcello Caetano, *Manuel de Ciencia Politica e Direito Constitucional,* 6th ed., 2 (Lisbon: Coimbra, 1970). Also Norman Blume, "Portugal Under Caetano," unpublished manuscript, 1974.

35. Cf. Lawrence Graham, "Portugal: The Bureaucracy of Empire." Also, Elena de la Souchère, "Caetano's Ambiguous Reforms," Le Monde Weekly Selection (18 February 1970); and Marvin Howe, "Portuguese Find the Spirit of Salazar Still Dominant," New York Times (20 August 1972). On the weakness of Caetano's succession and the failure of his reformist scenario, see Mario Soares, *Le Portugal Baillonné* (Paris: Calmann-Levy, 1972), pp. 259, 262, 274.

36. Silas Cerqueira, "L'Eglise Catholique et la dictature corporatiste portugaise," Revue Française de Science Politique 23 (June 1975): 473-513. Nevertheless, as Le Monde put it in a headline after the coup, "La hierarchie catholique reste en marge des transformations politiques," (23 May 1974).

37. Very few military officers held cabinet or higher administrative positions except in the military ministries, and even these were frequently held by civilians. Their proportional representation in both the National Assembly and the Corporative Chamber tended to decline over time (from 16.9% in 1934-38 to 9.6% in 1961-65). P. Schmitter, "Corporatist Representation and Public Policy in Authoritarian Portugal," p. 31a. Virtually all of the challenges to Salazar's personal hegemony arose from the ranks of the armed forces: Col. Norton de Matos, Gen. Humberto Delgado, Adm. José Mendes Cabeçadas, Capt. Henrique Galvão, Gen. Botellio Moniz—to name only the most prominent.

38. These frustrated coups are discussed in M. Soares, *La Portugal Baillonné*, pp. 119-20, 126-29. A list of them was published in Le Monde (2 April 1974). Several of the present civilian and military rulers of Portugal were co-conspirators as early as 1958. M. Niedergang, "L'armée portugaise ou la fascination du pouvoir," Le Monde (20-26 February 1975).

39. Salazar, doubling as Minister of National Defense at the time, telegraphed the governor of then Portuguese India: "I cannot conceive of a truce and I will not permit any Portuguese to be taken prisoners. No ship will surrender. I feel that there can only be victorious or dead soldiers and sailors." M. Soares, *La Portugal Baillonné*, p. 123. The officers were subsequently tried and cashiered in a public trial in Lisbon. The military hierarchy was well aware that defeat in Africa might result in their similarly becoming scapegoats. In one of its first memos to become public, the MFA protested against being harrassed and accused of cowardice by the civilian population of Beira in Mozambique, Le Monde (1 January 1974).

40. M. Niedergang, "L'armée portugaise."

41. Regular recruitment of officer candidates to the Military Academy, after the initial spurt in 1962, fell impressively; see Expresso (17 August 1970). Desertions were reaching impressive proportions. According to Le Monde Diplomatique (May 1974), 16,000 of the 30,000 called to arms had failed to show up.

42. Interview with Otelo Saraiva de Carvalho, Expresso (27 July 1974): 17-19.

43. Christopher Hitchens, "Portugal's Salvation Army," New Statesman (23 August 1974): 243. For another commentary on how the "social crisis" affected junior officers, see Thomas Bruneau, "The Portuguese Coup: Causes and Probable Consequences," The World Today (July 1974: 281-83).

44. This period from the end of December 1973 to April 1974 is still not clear. It does appear that the abortive coup of the colonialist "ultras," foiled by Spínola according to Le Monde (26 May 1974), both served to accelerate the timetable and to expand the demands of the junior officers of the MFA, and heightened resistance on the part of the military high command to Spínola. The permission to publish his book should probably be seen as an attempt by Caetano to build some countervailing centrist support in a rapidly deteriorating situation. See Le Monde Diplomatique (May 1974) and Le Monde (19 April 1974 and 17-18 March 1974).

45. João de Almada, "Reeleição de Thomaz descontentou generais." O Estado de São Paulo (30 July 1972).

46. These memoirs have not yet been published in Portugal. Excerpts and commentary about the Brazilian edition can be found in Expresso (30 November 1974 and 1 December 1974).

47. Mario Soares admits that Caetano's initial reformist image "demobilized" the opposition (*La Portugal Baillonné*, p. 280). Several commentators-participants have agreed that the political turning point for this effort at "renovation within continuity" came in 1971 with the gutting of the long-anticipated reform of the Press Law. See the interview of Sa Carneiro in Expresso (1 December 1974).

48. On the role of these *técnicos* and their failure, see Mario Soares, *La Portugal Baillonné*. The key group, SEDES—a sort of secular equivalent to the Spanish Opus Dei—was formed as a "civic association" in the late 1960s after meeting some resistance from the regime. Its activities declined somewhat in 1972-1974 but, since the coup, it has revived, recently declaring its support for an eventually (but not hurriedly) socialist Portugal.

49. The following lengthy quotation best captures, in my view, the "class-basis" and "developmental context" of the April coup:

> The MFA seems to have acted independently.... It is far-fetched to suppose that the army seized power under remote control from somewhere. Yet the Portuguese and international business did have a certain interest in putting a stop at this time to colonial warfare ... though (they) may not have intended the complete overthrow of the Salazar regime. The fact remains that there were certain parallels between the interests of the forces which helped to re-establish 'democratic' freedom and those of international capitalism. Internally, the small-scale capitalists who had provided Salazar's fascism with its most significant support were beginning to take a heavy battering. They were the victims of the economic concentration which was to the advantage of the large Portuguese and international groups who hold the real power in the country and whose policy was clearly to strengthen economic ties with the Common Market countries.... The policy of these major groups fitted in less and less easily with the fascist regime but would get on admirably with a bourgeoise democracy.... The change of political regime happened precisely at the time when the multinationals were systematically establishing themselves in the major sectors of the Portuguese economy [Jean-Pierre Dubois, "Portugal," Agenor, Nos. 45-46 (October 1974) 12-13].

PHILIPPE C. SCHMITTER is a professor of political science at the University of Chicago. His interest in corporatism and the comparative analysis of interest politics has led to recent study of Portugal and Switzerland. The present essay is part of a more extensive analysis of the Portuguese Revolution.

Review Article

The Liberation Army and the Chinese People

LYNN T. WHITE III
Princeton University

"Coups d'etat have today become a fad.... There have been 61 coups d'etat in the capitalist countries of Asia, Africa, and Latin America since 1960. Of these 61 coups, 56 were successful."
    Lin Piao, address to an enlarged meeting of
    the Politburo, May 18, 1966.

"The Chinese Red Army is an armed body for carrying out the political tasks of the revolution.... Without these objectives, fighting loses its meaning and the Red Army loses the reason for its existence."
    Mao Tse-tung at the Kut'ien Conference, December 1929.

Boorman, Scott A. THE PROTRACTED GAME: A WEI-CH'I INTERPRETATION OF MAOIST REVOLUTIONARY STRATEGY. New York: Oxford University Press, 1969, 242 pp., $7.50, paperback $2.50.

Cheng, J. Chester, ed. THE POLITICS OF THE CHINESE RED ARMY. Stanford: Hoover Institution, 1966, 776 pp., $35.00.

Fraser, Angus M. THE PEOPLE'S LIBERATION ARMY. New York: Crane, Russak, 1973, 62 pp., paperback $2.45.

George, Alexander L. THE CHINESE COMMUNIST ARMY IN ACTION. New York: Columbia University Press, 1967, 255 pp., $10.00.

Gittings, John. THE ROLE OF THE CHINESE ARMY. London: Oxford University Press, 1967, 331 pp. $9.50.

Griffith, Samuel B. II. *THE CHINESE PEOPLE'S LIBERATION ARMY.* New York: McGraw-Hill, 1967, 398 pp., $10.95.

Joffe, Ellis. *PARTY AND ARMY PROFESSIONALISM AND POLITICAL CONTROL IN THE CHINESE OFFICER CORPS.* Cambridge: Harvard University Press, 1967, 198 pp., paperback $4.50.

Kau, Ying-mao. *THE PEOPLE'S LIBERATION ARMY AND CHINA'S NATION-BUILDING.* White Plains: International Arts and Sciences Press, 1973, 407 pp., $15.00.

Whitson, William W., with Chen-hsia Huang. *THE CHINESE HIGH COMMAND: A HISTORY OF COMMUNIST MILITARY POLITICS, 1927-71.* New York: Praeger, 1973, 638 pp., $20.00.

Whitson, William W., ed. *THE MILITARY AND POLITICAL POWER IN CHINA IN THE 1970s.* New York: Praeger, 1972, 390 pp., $18.50.

How will the People's Liberation Army help shape future politics in China? There can scarcely be doubt that the PLA will play a major or even dominant role in determining the succession of personnel and policies after Chairman Mao's death. But any more detailed prediction must depend on research concerning both the internal structure of the PLA and its relations with Chinese society at large. Several good books on this subject have been published, and a review of them in the light of comparative ideas about military politics may be useful in clarifying emerging trends.

The question we must ask of these books is whether they show the relation between the structure and ethic of the PLA and its political prospects. Many books emphasize the norm of close army-people relations that was a tradition in Communist-managed parts of China even before 1949. Internal characteristics or distinctions within the army have also been studied, and the potential number of these distinctions is large. This article will review works that emphasize differences between "professionals" and "guerrillas" in the PLA, between various regional loyalty groups, between Party and army, and between "civilian" politicians and army commanders. Other analyses could be generated by other distinctions between the militia and the regular army, between Peking and the provinces, between political commissars and commanders, between the land, air, sea, and public security services, between generations of officers, between generals and colonels, between officers and men, between soldiers of different social class backgrounds or from different kinds of military academies, between northerners and southerners, ruralities and urbanites, inland Chinese or coastal cosmopolitans, and so on. There are various overlaps among these categories; so in principle we need not consider all of them. But the problem of measuring the extent of correlation among these groups in the PLA has not been solved. One author will describe the Chinese army by using one set of distinctions, another author may prefer a different set—and a problem of the literature as a whole is the lack of sure means to choose among them. Most writers on the subject have emphasized one categorical distinction over others when trying to define the political effects of the PLA.

SOLDIERS AND CIVILIANS: FIRST DISTINCTION

The external characteristics of the PLA are not typical of most armies. Ever since the failure of the Nanchang uprising (which was the Red Army's first operation after its founding on August 1, 1927), Communist Chinese military thinking has been closely related to civilian concerns. After the famous joining of forces under Mao Tse-tung and Chu Te at Chingkangshan in May 1928, a conflict developed between Mao's emphasis on small unit tactics and "professional" ideas about force deployment. The Kut'ien Conference of December 1929 did not finally solve this dilemma, but it provided a forum at which Mao could denounce the "purely military viewpoint."[1] Mao's dictum that "political power grows out of the barrel of a gun" represents him incompletely. He is also a revolutionary, and it matters what kind of politics grows out of the gun. At Kut'ien he argued, against a majority of his colleagues, that the new Red Army should be an economic as well as a military force, and ever since then he has been identified with movements to integrate the Red Army with Chinese Communist society while preserving social control over the military. Mao's theories on this bear at least some relation to Samuel Huntington's more general proposition that although militaries may help spur some kinds of social development, they cannot themselves provide legitimacy for complex government—as political parties are able to do.[2]

John Gittings' book *The Role of the Chinese Army* is largely a history of Mao's attempts to use the Red Army for quasi-civilian tasks. Communist strategy for beating the Kuomintang and Japan was an alternating one. Before the 1937 Battle of P'inghsingkuan against the Japanese, and again during the Hundred Regiments Offensive of 1940-1941 and the civil war in 1947-1949, the Communist army pressed its military operations energetically. The Korean War was a period of similar military activity. At other times, the work of the Red Army has been overwhelmingly social and political. To be sure, the PLA sometimes used guns during these basically nonmilitary periods, and Gittings gives fine descriptions of the consolidation efforts in places like Sinkiang,

Hainan, and Tibet during the early fifties. One of the main contributions of his book is to show that the periods of offensive were often periods of radical land policy. In September 1947, for example, directives called for equal distribution of land to peasants and to PLA soldiers, who were thus given tangible assets for which they would fight.

Gittings' account at many points suggests that the morale and capability of the Red Army has depended on the strength of its support among civilians. At no time has this been clearer than in the early 1960s, when crop failures and grain distribution problems following the Great Leap Forward affected army discipline. Rich documentation on this is available in copies of a *Bulletin of Activities* that was published by the General Political Department of the PLA and dispatched for confidential use to regiment levels. These papers were seized apparently by Khamba rebels in eastern Tibet during 1961, spirited out of China, released by the U.S. State Department, and published in translation by J. Chester Cheng.[3] The *Bulletin* contains a wealth of reports by top military leaders, who were then already worried about their age and consequent need to train successors to carry on their policies. Circulating memos are included which suggest that at least in the early sixties the downward flow of information within the command structure was generally more effective than the upward flow. Above all, the *Bulletin* makes clear that discipline in an army recruited from peasants is largely a function of the size of recent years' grain crops. Hunger during the atypical post-Leap period occasionally caused Chinese militiamen to raid warehouses, especially in Honan.[4] No other source documents so well the degree to which ordinary soldiers were aware of political problems both in their native villages and in the regions where they were stationed.

One of the least well-studied aspects of Chinese military politics is the role of the militia system.[5] Clearly the militia was a major means of PLA involvement in many Chinese work units, but the nature of this relationship has varied sharply from place to place. No comprehensive picture of it can be had from an analysis of central directives. During the Great Leap Forward, the "Everyone a Militiaman" movement was originally conceived to involve over 200 million Chinese peasants in military exercises. The size of this project would have precluded close supervision by the approximately 3 million PLA regular soldiers; but the campaign in any case fell far short of its goal, and the present size of the militia has been variously estimated at 12 to 15 million paramilitary irregulars, armed with about half as many rifles. PLA officers are assigned to lead intensive training at least in the "core militia" groups of factories and agricultural production brigades. Admission to the people's militia is by formal application, which must be approved by Party officials at a level above the applicant's unit. At least before the Cultural Revolution, activism in the militia was good for a worker's or student's career. Guns and ammunition for militia exercises were supplied by the "people's armed forces departments" that were associated with police officers under the concurrent orders of local governments and the "fourth service" public security forces of the PLA.[6] Militia squads were also often associated with trade unions. In Shanghai by 1966, they had an average of about ten reservists per squad, and large numbers of squads occasionally congregated for a wide variety of purposes.[7] They sponsored diverse activities including military summer camps and river swimming competitions, radio clubs, night schools for peasants, eyesight preservation campaigns, encouragement of youths' rustication, and shooting matches.[8] Little appears in the secondary English literature about these semi-civilian and semi-military activities, although local Chinese newspapers shortly before the Cultural Revolution are replete with information about them, and their importance for later events should by now be evident. Factory militias or their successor organizations often became gradualist, nonradical forces in the Cultural Revolution, and their previous links with PLA soldiers formed a basis for many new revolutionary committees. Demobilized soldiers who had returned to their original worksites (*fuyuan chunjen*) and demobilized soldiers who had been specifically assigned to work elsewhere on the basis of their military service (*chuanyeh chunjen*) apparently had somewhat different effects on these developments. The first group was generally more difficult for regular PLA officers to recruit for cooperation in restoring order after the Party's temporary demise, but the distinction between these two types has apparently not even been mentioned in the analytical English literature.

More than any other movement, the Cultural Revolution demonstrated the extent of interpenetration of the civilian and military sectors of Chinese politics. This mixing was not only a matter of fact, it was also a matter of ideals and symbols. When recently activized students began calling themselves Red "guards," and their younger comrades became "little Red soldiers," it seemed natural that a gas-meter repairmen's militia unit agreed to have itself named a "Mao Tse-tung Thought University."[9] Military units became civilianized as often as the reverse occurred.

Is the PLA a noncivilian entity? At least to make words clearer, we must ask this question. In some societies, the main impresarios, railroad companies, and frontier promoters have not been military. Even in China, these functions are not exclusively served by the PLA, but it plays a major part in performing them. These jobs are not strictly part of the traditional military mission, the monopoly of major arms. The army's participation in them has no necessary connection with its chain-of-command organization or its other intrinsic characteristics (its ethic of goals, uniforms, highly codified discipline, and so on). This "multifunctionality" may instead relate just to the fact that this is a large Chinese organization. Like other large Chinese establishments, it has a propensity for what Schurmann calls "gigantism"; it tends to diversify its operations into many fields.[10] If the PLA has become involved in a wide variety of economic, educational, artistic, and other enterprises, that fact may be less related to its specifically military nature than to the expectations placed on any organization that has resources in modern China.

It has often been thought that armies have characteristics which differentiate them from other parts of modernizing societies, and which make them relatively dynamic in demanding changes. According to Lucian Pye, they are by nature rival institutions; they are relatively immune from tests of immediate efficiency and they are widely expected to behave in unusual, noncivilian ways that are justified by the supposed greater efficacy of those manners in achieving their military aims.[11] But since Kut'ien, many of the organizational goals of the Chinese Red Army have become indistinguishable from civilian goals. The PLA's involvement in drama and land reclamation, morality, harvesting, and a myriad of other public workaday activities may weaken the possibility that civilians in China will consider the army to have a fully unique or specially effective style of politics. When a society becomes heavily "Praetorian" in its organization and goals, and an army becomes heavily civilianized, then the distinction between those two becomes a moot basis for predicting how the mixed whole will develop afterward. This relationship between organized soldiers and organized civilians in Chinese society is a single characteristic of both groups. A debate about whether traits "of" the army or "of" society most determine military intervention in politics will be difficult to conduct, since those traits cannot be separated from one another. That may be only a problem of analytical grammar. The close army-civilian relationship in China will nevertheless help as a unified datum to define the ways in which the PLA will participate in future politics. It is a fact that can be considered alongside other matters that are more strictly internal to the army.

PROFESSIONALS AND GUERRILLAS: SECOND DISTINCTION

Most studies of China's military have focused on the characteristics of the army elite. Some students of China have followed Alfred Vagt's classic distinction between the "rational military mind" and the "spirit of militarism"[12] and have seen a basic difference between "professional soldiers" in the modern PLA and "veteran guerrillas" who spent many years in the bush during the Japanese occupation and before. As Morris Janowitz has pointed out, the combat soldier is the antithesis of Weber's organization man, and bureaucratic professionalism does not have an uncontested claim to legitimacy in most armies.[13] Military work is not inherently routinized, self-contained, or most effective when it follows rigid procedures. Planned divisions of labor break down in battle situations.

A considerable part of the available English literature on the PLA concerns the combat effectiveness of that organization and the extent to which professionalism or guerrillaism may affect that capability. A recent small book by Colonel Angus M. Fraser is basically a list of the PLA'S military resources with a gloss of speculations on how they can be used in offensive and defensive operations. A deeper and longer study has been made by General Samuel Griffith, whose history of the battles and structure of the PLA includes much material that is useful for political analysis.[14] Griffith attaches more military importance to the individual personalities of commanding officers than a nonprofessional easily finds credible, but his data on the decisions and politics of the PLA during the Korean conflict provide a solid basis for approaching the most important challenge Mao has ever faced from "professional" soldiers.

Traditional deception tactics, as expounded in the Chou Dynasty classic *Sun Tzu* or in Mao's 1938 essay "On Protracted War,"[15] were before Korea the content of the professionalism of most Chinese commanders. The liveliest English description of these methods, in Scott Boorman's *The Protracted Game: A Wei-ch'i Interpretation of Maoist Revolutionary Strategy*, has many implications for politics as well as for war. Boorman argues that guerrilla tactics have been understood by the Chinese largely in terms of the formal rules of the game that in Japanese and English is usually called *go*. This analogy allows great possibilities for intellectual theater, and none of them are missed. A section of the book is labeled "The Kiangsi Period as a Wei-ch'i Opening"; another is headed "The Game in Central China"; and a map is titled "The Manchurian Board." But the bulk of this highly imaginative book is a chronological account of Chinese Communist battles from the beginning to liberation, with running simulations on the *wei-ch'i* board. Boorman codifies some of the principles of the game and contrasts them with Western rules of war, and particularly with chess. The encirclement of territory wins in *wei-ch'i*; the capture of pieces, in chess. The upshot for political analysis is more suggestive than specific, but that may be all we can ask from a game simulation. Boorman's execution of the project is brilliant, and his book is a circus in print.

As Ellis Joffe makes clear in his publication *Party and Army,* the Korean War greatly accelerated a change of reliance in the PLA from guerrilla-enveloping tactics to more fixed battle lines and larger weapons and formations. Although political loyalty certainly remained a requirement for officership after that war, educational qualifications were also increasingly important. Dozens of new military academies turned out a large cadre of professional officers, most of whom were outranked by older soldiers with experience in the Yenan period. But since senior officers also had differences of commitment among themselves about the relative advantages of encircling warfare and capturing warfare, this split in fact permeated the army. Although writers such as Alexander George and Samuel Griffith emphasize different sets of evidence on the extent to which the "Chinese People's Volunteers" were reduced in military effectiveness by the time the Korean armistice negotiations began,[16] there seems to be little disagreement that the war between China and America was a traumatic experience in strategic terms for both armies. The military spirit of the PLA in this war was rather well maintained by a system of political officers, intensive ethical indoctrination, and "3-by-3" squad organization that George describes vividly on the basis of interviews with Chinese POW's in Korea. On the other hand, when the "U.N." forces learned to absorb the shock of "human sea" tactics and then to counterattack, the previous Chinese policy of using large, lightly armed forces lost credit in Chinese eyes. That is why the Korean War clearly boosted "professionalism" in the PLA. Soviet aid to the air branch also gave some Chinese officers a taste for modern weaponry. The modernizers espoused a new version of the old substance-use (*t'i-yung*) dichotomy that had engaged Confucian modernizers in the nineteenth century. "Professionals" now claimed that the people's army would not lose its essence if it became a "tiger growing wings."

Part of the subsequent history of the PLA can be explained in terms of the Korean experience. In 1954 the last of the military-dominated "great administrative areas" in various parts of China were abolished, systematic conscription was introduced, and a more centralized structure was established under a new ministry of defense. The next year, ranks were instituted and new awards and medals were awarded for past service.

In 1956 the General Political Department of the PLA ordered officers with the rank of major or higher to complete five specified courses within the same number of years, and to take exams on set subjects that had to be passed eventually. Most of the materials for these courses were political. The requirement implied a need in many units to build more ideological expertise, which might allow the army to function effectively without close integrative or affective relations between different levels of the hierarchy.[17] The consequences of this and many other policies for "guerrilla" or "professional" viewpoints during the mid-fifties are less clear than they may seem at first. Certainly the "professionals" pressed for expensive equipment procurement, but long-run and short-run investments for that purpose are inherently different from one another; so those divisions may have been quite complex. Close political control in the army was certainly a prime method of "guerrillas" in small units during the Red Army's past wars, but the extent of their support for centralized political control at this time is less obvious. Even the role reversal and rustication (*hsiafang*) of officers during 1957-1958 had effects that cut many ways. This was certainly a nonprofessional policy in that it mixes commanders with privates; but everyone involved still knew who was who, and the main effect may have been to move military bureaucrats from their paper-shuffling jobs at desks to more obviously military work.[18]

The "professional" versus "guerrilla" difference in modern China has never been a simply army versus Party difference. As Joffe himself points out, all the important professionals have been long-standing, honored Party members. The most clear-cut policy distinctions that cause divisions along this line can occur only at high political levels. The details of the most spectacular instance need not be given here. Defense Minister P'eng Te-huai was dismissed in 1959 at the Lushan Plenum of the Central Committee for his vocal opposition to the economic failures of Mao Tse-tung's Great Leap policies and their effects in the army. Lin Piao replaced him as defense minister, and personnel were replaced in all the highest posts that must mediate issues which arise between "professionals" and "guerrillas." The new defense minister brought fresh men into the sensitive offices of chief of staff, director of the political department, and director of the rear services department.

In the early sixties the PLA under Lin Piao became even more active in social affairs than it had been before. Already by March 1960, meetings were being held even among militia units at the most local level to encourage "five good" model soldiers, who would be capable "with guns, with pens, and in the fields."[19] By 1964 ranks were eliminated along with distinctions in military dress. The abolition of ranks may have served "guerrillaism" concretely by eliminating forced promotion or retirement ages for major generals and all inferior officers, thus allowing more old men with Yenan experience to remain on active duty.

Two events of the mid-sixties, U.S. involvement in Vietnam and China's explosion of a nuclear bomb, affected the political role of the PLA in opposite ways. P'eng Te-huai's fall had not spelled the end of sympathy in high Party circles for his policy positions. The removal of Public Security Minister Lo Jui-ch'ing in late 1965 may or may not have been related to factional links with the USSR, but clearly it resurrected the P'eng issue and was related to strategic debates surrounding the PLA's ability to react (once again) to the potential of U.S. forces operating near China's land border.[20] Perceptions of this new foreign threat temporarily strengthened the arguments of "professionals" who called for more expensive weaponry. But in the same period, local evidence indicates that intensive political indoctrination campaigns were beginning to produce more boredom than loyalty among troops. The hagiology of models and slogans under Lin Piao's sponsorship had already become complex and even esoteric. "Insufficient class sentiments and inadequate consciousness" was reported among PLA air troops stationed in Shanghai, because "the aim of their learning is not explicit enough. They have no clear way to use Mao Tse-tung's thought to improve their own ideas or guide their actions."[21] By the autumn harvest of 1966, when the Cultural Revolution had begun in earnest, the army's political education campaign moved more than ever before out of barracks. In the Shanghai Garrison, for example, ground, sea, and air forces were all ordered to "bring their *Quotations of Chairman Mao* to the fields in the people's communes and publicize the sayings of Chairman Mao while they do work."[22] A relatively relaxed defense strategy based on the prediction that American forces would not move north from Vietnam, prevailed very soon after Lo's downfall.

During this time also, Chinese nuclear bombs afforded increasing proof against a major land invasion from abroad. This technical development had exactly the opposite political effect from that of the PLA's professionalization in the Korean War. The existence of Chinese atomic weapons strengthened the hands of political commissars and civilians who insisted that China, with inexpensive procurement of media weapons, could still viably maintain independence from other large states, especially from the USSR. Nuclear weapons made the strictly military role of many PLA troops less urgent than it would otherwise have been. The low-level political functions of the army could thus become correspondingly more important.

The best current book on the PLA, a symposium edited by William Whitson that is titled *The Military and Political Power in China in the 1970s,* contains articles by Joseph Heinlein, Harvey Nelsen, and Paul Elmquist which all offer data to confirm the PLA's major commitment to domestic goals of policing and political management. The historian Edward Dreyer also offers a chapter that is rich with precedents showing how traditional Chinese regimes preferred whenever possible to use troops for preserving order within the country rather than fighting external powers. The bomb had the paradoxical effect of narrowing Chinese perceptions of what an effective strictly military profession would be, and so of allowing a reversion to more traditional norms for soldiers' work. The most sophisticated development in the profession strengthened the policy arguments of "guerrillas."

LOYALTY GROUPS: THIRD DISTINCTION

The PLA has many political levels,[23] and their actual interests may concern personal careers and civil politics as much as military victories in a war that is not being fought. The PLA's political behavior in its broad social setting cannot be fully derived from its military goals, because in fact its sections have other goals too.

The most important description of the PLA based on the nonmilitary functions of its parts has come out of the massive researches of Colonel William W. Whitson. His book *The Chinese High Command* indicates that most Chinese Communist army officers received their formative career experiences in military units that have cooperated in relatively stable patterns from the times of their founding probably to the present. More than most writers in the field, Whitson presents us with various alternative analyses concurrently. For example, he has done considerable work to suggest that the Chinese officer corps of 1970 could be discussed in terms of eleven military "generations" that joined the PLA at times of specific crises. But the largest and most important formations that Whitson emphasizes are the five field armies that occupied large areas of China at the time of liberation.[24] Whitson indicates that even after the 1954 centralization under a new Chinese constitution, the five field armies remained the prime political units in provinces which they had occupied during the civil war. According to this theory, field armies competed with each other by sending observers to each others' areas. Relatively prosperous or crucial military regions, especially those centered at Nanking, Shenyang, and Peking, received more such representatives than did other regions.

Whitson thus uses personnel changes as evidence of competition among the field armies. But William Parish, challenging Whitson's ideas, proposes a random migration model to explain these same changes at least from the mid-fifties to 1967. Parish objects that Whitson cites both personnel stability and personnel change as proofs of a power struggle among the various field armies' loyalty groups; so there would be no way to controvert the hypothesis of field army rivalry on the basis of such data. Parish's argument does not disprove Whitson's thesis; it asserts only that the emphasis on field army politics has not been adequately established for the late fifties and early sixties. But then, Parish turns around and offers additional data to show that the field armies may indeed have been important political entities during the Cultural Revolution! He relies especially on Chief of Staff Yang Ch'eng-wu's favoritism for clients in the Fifth Field Army. When standard rules of predictable behavior broke down during the Cultural Revolution, underlying loyalty systems from earlier years may indeed have become important, according to Parish. He posits a bureaucratic politics model along the lines of Crozier, Blau, or Downs, under which "forgotten personal relationships" are resurrected throughout an organization when formal, vertical ties disintegrate very quickly—as happened to some extent even in the army during the Cultural Revolution. Whitson can well accept this much at least. There may be some inconsistency in Parish's doubts about the basic political importance of the old field armies before 1967 and his documented assertion of their reemergence after that. But the relatively sophisticated debate that he initiated concerning regional command appointments in China might be read with benefit by students of other militaries. The points at which Parish, Whitson, David Goodman, and other participants do not conflict are related to the general policy cycle in China. Whitson's main idea (that the army faction systems exist) and Parish's (that their salience may depend on political instability) both survive the controversy. Periods of radical change tend to intensify long-standing emotional loyalty bonds relative to newer, more legal-rational ones, so that the essential characteristics of military politics are closely related to the speed with which the kaleidoscope of revolution is turned by the whole Chinese leadership.[25]

Further confirmation for these ideas comes from China recently. The stunning shift of regional commanders that was announced at the beginning of 1974 certainly indicated that the central Chinese government had influence within any loyalty systems. It was almost as if Premier Chou had read Colonel Whitson's book, was disturbed by the implications, and decided on a practical critique.[26] If the eight military region commanders who were transferred had instead been purged, we might speculate about the central government's continuing fear of a junta after Lin's fall. But the authorities in Peking apparently had no such lack of confidence. Hsu Shih-yu was transferred out of the rich Nanking Military Region—long the main base of his Third Field Army—to head the Canton Military Region, a traditional base of the Fourth Army, which is in national terms also significant. Neither his old job nor his new one is a minor sinecure. Ch'en Hsi-lien, who had since 1959 commanded the politically strategic and economically prosperous Shenyang Military Region, was transferred to the central command at Peking. No full list is needed here to indicate the sweep of these transfers. They indicate that China is not about to fly apart centrifugally because of rivalries among military regions. They underline that all these commanders are patriotic Chinese. But they do not discredit the notion that there was, and may to some limited extent still be, an underlying system of regionally based factions within the PLA.[27]

FORMAL AND INFORMAL ORGANIZATION: FOURTH DISTINCTION

We have thus far been discussing approaches to the PLA that are based at least implicitly on assumptions about the organizational goals of the army or its parts. But analysis by functions is not the only way to view the situation. The internal structure of the PLA can also be approached with an expectation that its politics will follow to some extent the obvious official hierarchy and rules under which it is formally constituted.

Harvey Nelsen argues that China's military regions are not mainly troop commands, but are mainly administrative units for logistics, training, and other purposes that are subsidiary to major policies. Many orders from regional or local "commanders" must be approved from higher levels—often in Peking—before they are binding on lower units. In addition, the six air districts and three fleet headquarters, all partly under the jurisdiction of Peking, are mostly not coterminous with land army regions. The bureaucratic relationships between military and civilian administrators in many areas still further reduce the independence of local commanders, according to Nelsen.[28] This argument derives from an insistence on studying legal as well as informal patterns of military politics. Another more circumspect paradigm along somewhat similar lines can be found in an article by John Gittings,[29] who points out that the Party and the army have a long history of institutional rivalry in China, but the close personal relationships between civilian and military leaders in many parts of China have often tended to weaken the army as a separate institution. When the Cultural Revolution began, a central "Maoist" faction (including Defense Minister Lin) relied on the PLA to "support the left." But apparently the regional commanders in fact were less enthusiastic to do that than to confirm stable powers in the new revolutionary committees where they had representation. Their main institutional rival, the Party, was in shambles, but the PLA had scant will or central coordination for purposes either of opposing or supporting the revolutionary leadership in Peking. The various armies could then threaten no coups, because they were so enmeshed in local bureaucracies and rivalries that no national stage had been built for anything like a dramatic, "praetorian" coup d'etat.

Nelsen and Gittings thus argue in different ways that the PLA is a weak institution, both at local levels and also nationally. It is weak because of a contradiction between its actual dispersion and its centralized formal rules; it was weakened during the fifties by the resistance of guerrilla veterans to what some officers considered to be the lessons of the Korean War; it was weakened in the sixties by Lin Piao's involvement of the PLA with local Party committees and by the lack of a representative center; and it is weakened now by the emergence of a more unified post-Cultural Revolution bureaucracy in Peking. But the focus of these arguments is on the continuing organizational diffuseness of the army, not on the changing succession of issues that give rise to it.

Whitson's symposium in *The Military and Political Power in China in the 1970s* contains more information on organization in the PLA than has previously been brought together. This book contains nineteen different contributions—too many to characterize separately here with any justice. Whitson is in the admirable position of having sponsored some eloquent implicit criticisms of his own ideas. Chapters by James Jordan, Glenn Dick, Joseph Heinlein, John Coon, and Harvey Nelsen all use different frameworks that are at odds partially with the loyalty group approach. Together with some other contrasting chapters that will be mentioned, they form the most detailed and varied account of the relation between the PLA and Chinese society that can currently be found between two covers.

The topic of diffuse boundaries between army and Party is hardly a new one in discussions of Chinese politics. Trotsky's commissar system was introduced by the KMT's National Revolutionary Army, and the Whampoa Military Academy taught the necessity of political controls over the military in preparation for the Northern Expedition. During the Korean War, the power of political commissars was so great that military orders had to be signed by them as well as by commanders, whereas political directives did not need commanders' countersignatures. If the commander of a unit became a casualty, the political officer (rather than the deputy commander) assumed charge. Party committees exist in PLA units at least from the regiment level up. During the period of Lin Piao's reforms, each company was also supposed to have a Party branch committee, and each platoon, a Party small group.[30] "Political work conferences" were held regularly, and Party cadres were often "sent down" to the army. Other kinds of controls were imposed by a hierarchy of "political departments" in regiments and higher levels, and sometimes below that by the management committees of official soldiers' clubs especially at the company level. In military districts which comprise one or a few provinces, a first Party secretary from the dominant provincial apparatus (or after 1966, the chairman of a provincial revolutionary committee) almost always served concurrently as the first political commissar, or in border areas as the commander, of the area's garrison.

The Cultural Revolution has therefore sometimes been described as a PLA reaction to Party interference. As early as May 24, 1966, Radio Peking quoted a political instructor of an army company in that city as saying that

> We must warn [Party secretary] Teng T'o and his ilk that the right to "contend" is not allowed in the PLA, and the people will wipe out those who dare to stick their noses into the army under the pretext of "contention."

But Teng T'o was high in the official Party apparatus at Peking; and according to the old rules, he ought to have had influence over the military unit involved. The fifteenth article of the Sixteen-Point Decision of the Central Committee on August 8, 1966, specifically exempted the PLA from being under the jurisdiction even of the Cultural Revolution Group of the Party that Chiang Ch'ing and her comrades directed, although this group took great liberties in advising all other kinds of agencies in China. It had been determined that the PLA was "a proletarian army personally created by Chairman Mao," having "the obligation as well as favorable conditions for learning from Chairman Mao's works a little better than other units."[31]

By autumn 1966, Lin Piao initiated a "call" for "discussion and application meetings" (*chiangyung hui*) to be organized by PLA units in schools, factories, and agricultural brigades, near barracks.[32] This particular foray of the military into low-level civilian politics has apparently been neglected thus far in secondary English literature, although it represents an early use of the PLA command structure to coordinate the Cultural Revolution and it came at an obviously crucial time.

The PLA did not enjoy internal unity during the Cultural Revolution. Different garrisons were included to intervene or to restrain themselves according to their own dictates. Many directives were sent down from Peking on the need to "support the left," but they were not followed in any standard way.[33] Formal organization certainly has some effect on PLA behavior; but like the three other major categories of analysis discussed earlier, it alone will not suffice to generate a simple explanation of the Chinese army's participation in politics.

REACTIVE MILITARISM: ANALYTIC CATEGORIES AND POLITICAL PROBLEMS

The most recent major book in the field is *The People's Liberation Army and China's Nation-Building* by Ying-mao Kau.[34] The bulk of this volume consists of translations of Chinese statements about the PLA's role in the cultural social, and economic spheres; but the heart of the book is an introduction by the editor. Kau begins in a somewhat conventional manner by contrasting the functions and structures of the PLA and Western militaries. The striking thing about the PLA is that it is already so thoroughly involved in society. Documents from Kut'ien onward are presented to show the continuing fusion of military with political work. More important, this book begins to suggest a basis for building theory which may allow more dynamic use of the various categorical distinctions that have been discussed above as dominant variables in past analyses of the PLA. Kau follows Morris Janowitz in using the term "reactive militarism" to describe a syndrome by which civilian politicians recruit the military to help solve social problems that would be intractable without army assistance.[35] Revolutionary regimes are prone to reactive militarism, because their commitment to change gives rise to social enemies whom the military is needed to keep in check. The general policy cycle in China may therefore have a tendency to involve the army increasingly in politics at all levels. Ting Wang and Parris Chang in Whitson's symposium present new evidence, including new statistics, to show how far the militarization of Chinese politics had already proceeded by mid-1971. This trend itself is a major datum about Chinese military politics that must be explained. Janowitz's idea suggests that analyses of the PLA might be made more dynamic if this revolutionary government's goals of change were taken more fully into account.

Definitions of the PLA's future role must rely on studies of political problems, not just on analyses by categories. The fine essay by Harry Harding in the Whitson collection suggests this approach, because it deals with fluctuating factions of statesmen in three problem periods when concrete decisions had to be made about the PLA. Categorical distinctions are referred to mainly in terms of the specific issues that arose in

1955-1956, 1959, and 1967. Another more limited implicit application of this approach is Charles Horner's contribution to the same book, which foretells that various parts of the PLA may increasingly diverge in terms of their work styles and penetration of general politics. In particular, the small but important Second Artillery (China's nuclear force) may remain highly professionalized, while the bulk of the army may continue to operate broadly in social affairs and so subject itself to open opposition from civilian interests. This type of approach relates the PLA's role to issues, needs, and functions in the least constricted sense.

CONCLUSION: THE NATURE OF A CHINESE COUP

What do the available books tell us about whether there will be a coup in China after Mao's death? The PLA's present political involvement is great enough that anyone's answer to the question must be restricted by the reason he gives for that current fact. Kau's book shows more clearly than any other the "multifunctionality" and "structural diffuseness" of the PLA in many contexts. He contends that the April 1969 designation of Lin Piao as official successor may have been "forced" on Mao due to the growing influence of the army. He describes the August 1970 Lushan Plenum as nearly a repeat performance of the 1959 one; civilian factions once again asserted their power, this time against commanders who demanded that Lin Piao be installed as Chairman of the Republic. This insistence, that a junta be legitimized in effect, was reportedly voted down on Mao's instructions. According to Kau's description, early in 1971 some commanders began conspiring to make a coup; but they waited too long without acting, and by September their plot was uncovered before they had struck. Thomas Robinson's chapter in the Whitson symposium argues for an opposite view that emphasizes the public strength of the Mao-Lin alliance at least through 1970 and possibly even to the time of Lin's death. Indeed the attempted coup of 1971 threatened the stability of the military-civilian balance in China; but in fact this movement failed. Lin Piao was unable to coordinate enough support quickly in the army to assume power. Reliable contemporary evidence on the affair is still in short supply, but most interpretations would be consistent with the idea that it is not easy to identify the army's interests in China solely with soldiers, or civilian interests only with nonmilitary politicians. Kau tells us that "The pattern of military development in China since 1958 has vividly illustrated the dangers inherent in the Maoist concept of the army's extra-military role. . . ."[36] But when an army has such variegated interests, what precisely are those "dangers"?

After Lin's fall, a campaign was launched within the PLA to encourage study of the "Three Main Rules of Discipline" and the "Eight Points for Attention"—i.e., to encourage soldiers' courtesy to civilians. Western liberal notions about the proper narrow role of the armed forces in society may have somewhat discouraged military high-handedness, or even coups, in some non-Western countries like India; but in the Chinese context, these liberal ideas are certainly not recommended on the basis of their origins. The common denominator among the various approaches to PLA politics that involve categorical distinctions is that they describe norms built up among soldiers during shared experiences dealing with specific problems. A dynamic theory is needed to show how all these distinctions arise, how they change, how they should be weighted in importance, and how they relate to each other. Such a theory must probably be based on a study of issues, and on all kinds of them. If Whitson's exemplary work with several sorts of distinctions can be paralleled by research along other lines, and if there is a continuing effort to weigh the effectiveness of different analyses in changing times, then the present good literature in this field can improve further.

The PLA is already more involved in Chinese society than are some militaries after they conduct coups. S. E. Finer proposed a four-part typology of "political cultures" that might be generated out of different levels of military intervention in politics. In "mature" cultures, armies are only able to influence politics procedurally; they are able to apply more pressure in "developed" cultures; they act as king-makers among civilian politicians in "low" culutres; and they take direct charge from civilians only in "minimal" political cultures.[37] But to the extent that the civilian-military distinction has much importance in contemporary China at all, it could be as easily argued that civilians have brought soldiers to power as that the military men themselves have seized it. Nonsoldiers' proof against coup-type movements in modern China does not lie in any tradition of legitimacy for civilian leadership there. On the contrary, it lies in the Communist tradition that soldiers are supposed to hold explicitly nonmilitary interests as primary. The purpose of political officers is constantly to remind army men that their "profession" is not a narrow one. Many of those soldiers believe that they will not be effective, even in fighting, unless their motives relate to China's general social life. The Communist revolution was itself a kind of coup; and the main question is whether it will continue with its recent intensity, or subside. The answer to that question may most determine the type of army involvement in China's future politics. However that may turn out, the current set of men with civilian interests who call themselves soldiers of the Chinese PLA are unlikely to regard any government over them as fully legitimate unless they participate in constituting it.

NOTES

1. The best general history of the PLA in any language, whose specific theses will be treated below, is William W. Whitson, with Chen-hsia Huang, *The Chinese High Command.*
2. Cf. Samuel P. Huntington, *Political Order in Changing Societies* (New Haven: Yale University Press, 1968). ch. 4.
3. *The Politics of the Chinese Red Army: A Translation of the Bulletin of Activities of the People's Liberation Army* (Stanford: Hoover Institution, 1966).
4. One cannot help wondering whether the U.S. government's classification rules have been more easily waived in the past to release valuable documents with this viewpoint than other documents that may also have come out of China, but with conclusions more favorable to the People's Republic of China.
5. Gittings, op. cit., pp. 202-204, is still one of the few treatments in hardback. Harvey Nelsen's article in William W. Whitson, ed., *The Military and Political Power in China in the 1970s,* esp. pp. 136-141, contains considerable information. There are also scattered journal articles; but the Chinese militia will hopefully receive more extensive treatment in the future. The information in this paragraph is from the author's own research.
6. Interviews by the author of a Cantonese ex-cadre and ex-CCP member in Hong Kong, 1971.
7. Hsinmin wanpao (New People's Evening News), Shanghai (hereafter HMWP), January 18, 1966, p. 1.
8. HMWP, May 24, 1964, p. 4; July 9, 1964, p. 2; and April 28, 1965, p. 2; and Jenmin jihpao (People's Daily), Peking, November 19, 1966, p. 2.
9. HMWP, August 7, 1966, p. 1.
10. Cf. Franz Schurmann, *Ideology and Organization in Communist China* (Berkeley): University of California Press, 1965), pp. 298-307.
11. Lucian W. Pye, *Aspects of Political Development: An Analytic Study* (Boston: Little, Brown, 1966), pp. 178-179.
12. *A History of Militarism* rev. ed., originally published in 1937 (New York: Meridian Books, 1959).
13. "Hierarchy and Authority in the Military Establishment," in Amitai Etzioni, ed., *Complex Organizations: A Sociological Reader* (New York: Holt, Rinehart, and Winston, 1961), pp. 210-211. Cf. also Schurmann, op. cit., p. 237.
14. Samuel B. Griffith II, *The Chinese People's Liberation Army.* Both General Griffith and Colonel Fraser are retired from the U.S. Marine Corps; Colonel Whitson, mentioned above and below, is retired from the U.S. Army.

15. Cf. Sun Tzu, *The Art of War,* trans. Samuel B. Griffith II (Oxford: Clarendon Press, 1963), and Mao Tse-tung, *Selected Military Writings of Mao Tse-tung* (Peking: Foreign Language Press, 1963). Mao summarizes his tactics in sixteen words: The enemy advances, we withdraw; the enemy tarries, we harass; the enemy tires, we fight; the enemy withdraws, we pursue."

16. Cf. Alexander L. George, *The Chinese Communist Army in Action,* pp. 11-12, and Samuel B. Griffith II, op. cit., pp. 169-171.

17. Some of these ideas are derived or distorted generally from Schurmann, op. cit.

18. Suggested by Hsinwen jihpao (News Daily), Shanghai (hereafter HWJP), January 11, 1958, p. 2.

19. Cf. HMWP, March 13, 1960, p. 4.

20. For a view linking Lo with the Soviets, cf. the first version of a hypothesis by Uri Ra'anan, "Peking's Foreign Policy 'Debate,' 1965-1966," in Tang Tsou, ed., *China in Crisis: China's Policies in Asia and America's Alternatives* (Chicago: University of Chicago Press, 1968), pp. 23-71. Or see his slightly revised later version, "Chinese Factionalism and Sino-Soviet Relations," Current History 59, 349 (September 1970): 134-141. For another analysis, which generally agrees regarding the role of the United States, but disagrees regarding the Soviets, cf. Harry Harding, Jr., and Melvin Gurtov, *The Purge of Lo Jui-ch'ing: The Politics of Chinese Strategic Planning* (Santa Monica: RAND Corporation, 1971).

21. HMWP, April 17, 1965, p. 4.

22. Shanghai wanpao (Shanghai Evening News), Shanghai (hereafter SHWP), October 11, 1966, p. 2.

23. For a rather abstruse definition of the term "political level," cf. White, "Shanghai's Polity in Cultural Revolution," in John Wilson Lewis, ed., *The City in Communist China* (Stanford: Stanford University Press, 1971).

24. Cf. Whitson, *The Chinese High Command,* op. cit., a 638-page volume. Major chapters are devoted to detailed histories of each of the field armies. Whitson's book is nearly definitive on such subjects. The main commanders and locations of the field armies are so important in Whitson's analysis that they should be listed here: First Field Army, P'eng Te-Huai, Northwest; Second Field Army, Liu Po-ch'eng, "Central" China (a swath of provinces from Honan through Szechuan to Tibet); Third Field Army, Ch'en Yi, East China; Fourth Field Army, Lin Piao, Northeast and also Hunan-Kwangtung-Kwangsi; Fifth, or so-called "Headquarters," Field Army, Nieh Jung-chen, North China (i.e., Peking, Hopei, and Shansi). Each army ran a single military region, except the Fourth Field Army which had two regions centered in Shenyang and Canton. The first postliberation "civilian" governments of China were also established in these six regions.

25. Cf. William L. Parish, "Factions in Chinese Military Politics," China Quarterly (hereafter CQ) 56 (October-December 1973): 667-699; also William W. Whitson, "Comment: Statistics and the Field Army Loyalty System," CQ 57 (January-March 1974): 146 f., and the immediately following comments by David S. G. Goodman and again William L. Parish. I have benefited in this section from reading an unpublished paper by Peter R. Wang, "Alternative Perceptions of the PLA," submitted in July 1974 to Professor John Starr at the University of California, Berkeley.

26. But cf. *The Chinese High Command,* conclusion on page 557, to show that Whitson was not unaware of the possibility of such a civilian "coup." This author's practical insights are in fact less wedded to the field army analysis than many of his sentences might suggest.

27. An interesting article written after these changes, but clearly concerned that they may be inconsistent with Whitson's logics, is Allen S. H. Kong, "Comradeship in Arms: An Analysis of Power through Associations in the CPLA—February 1970 to February 1974," Asian Survey 14, 7 (July 1974); 663-677.

28. "Military Forces in the Cultural Revolution," CQ 51 (July-September 1972): 444-474.

29. "Army-Party Relations in the Light of the Cultural Revolution," in John Wilson Lewis, ed., *Party Leadership and Revolutionary Power in China* (Cambridge: Cambridge University Press, 1970), pp. 373-403.

30. Chalmers A. Johnson, "Lin Piao's Army and its Role in Chinese Society: Part I," Current Scene 4, 13 (1966): 5 f.

31. New China News Agency, Peking, May 4, 1966.

32. SHWP, October 11, 1966, p. 1; November 16, 1966, p. 3, and November 20, 1922, p. 2.

33. Cf. Oskar Weggel, "The PLA in the Cultural Revolution: Grass-roots Level Organization and Mass Work," Revue du Sud-est Asiatique et de l'Extreme Orient 2 (1969): 243-254; Ellis Joffe, "The Chinese Army in the Cultural Revolution: The Politics of Intervention," Current Scene 8, 18 (December 7, 1970): 1-25; and especially Thomas W. Robinson, "The Wuhan Incident: Local Strife and Provincial Rebellion During the Cultural Revolution," CQ 47 (July-September 1971): 413-438. An example of Cultural Revolution group member Yao Wen-yuan's advice to an air commander can be found in White, "Shanghai's Polity in Cultural Revolution," op. cit., p. 331.

34. The Bibliography at the end of Kau's book includes many Japanese and Chinese articles, as well as English ones. It is the best recent list of the literature which this reviewer has seen.

35. A similar point is made in Ellis Joffe's fine article, "The Chinese Army after the Cultural Revolution: The Effects of Intervention," CQ 55 (July-September 1973): esp. p. 452.

36. Kau, op. cit., p. xlv.

37. S. E. Finer, *The Man on Horseback: The Role of the Military in Politics* (London, 1962).

LYNN T. WHITE III is a professor of politics and government at Princeton University.